What Does The
Holy Spirit
Do In Our Lives?

What Does The Holy Spirit Do In Our Lives?
© 2005 RBC Ministries

Discovery House Publishers is affiliated with
RBC Ministries, Grand Rapids, Michigan 49512

Cover Photo: Terry Bidgood

Scripture taken from the New King James Version,
©1982 by Thomas Nelson, Inc. Used by permission.

Printed in the United States of America
05 06 07 08 09 / DP / 10 9 8 7 6 5 4 3 2 1

Contents

Preface

In recent years the work and person of the Holy Spirit has been a subject of great debate and confusion. While in the midst of the controversy, however, it is all too easy to lose sight of the powerful ministry of the Spirit in the life of the believer. In part to respond to the focal points of the debate, and in part to redirect our attention to the elements of the ministry of the Spirit that are beyond debate, we have collected four of our *Discovery Series* booklets to help us think through the profound question, "What does the Holy Spirit do in our lives?"

As you give thoughtful consideration to the biblical themes explored in this book, it is our sincere desire that your life and heart will be blessed and enriched by the powerful presence of the Third Person of the Godhead—God the Holy Spirit. May His work and ministry become an ever-increasing impact on our relationship with Christ and with our heavenly Father.

Bill Crowder
Director of Publications, RBC Ministries

ONE

THE PROMISE
OF THE SPIRIT

The message on the T-shirt said, "It's a Holy Spirit thing—you wouldn't understand." There can be little doubt that the doctrine of the Holy Spirit has been the seedbed for an enormous amount of misunderstanding during the last 35 years, and it's a subject every Christian needs to understand.

Clearing away some of the current confusion is our goal as we look at our Lord's promise of the Spirit in John 14. His words provide answers to such questions as: Who is the Holy Spirit? Is the Spirit a person or a power? Why did the Spirit come? What difference does all of this make to me?

As we turn to Jesus' words for answers, it's my desire that we will not only understand the person and ministry of the Holy Spirit, but that we will embrace His presence in our lives.

Bill Crowder

WHERE CAN WE TURN?

A well-used bag of golf clubs slouches at the bottom of the stairs, just where he left it. She had given it to him for his 50th birthday. How can she part with something he enjoyed so much? And what should she do with his wallet and clothes? And what about the lawnmower? How will she pay the bills he always paid, or run the business he knew inside and out? Whom can she turn to now that he's gone? Will she ever be able to trust anyone again?

Some of her questions are similar to those being asked by the grieving followers of a rabbi whom many believed to be the messiah of Israel. Rabbi Menachem Mendel Schneerson was the leader of the Lubavitch movement (a global Jewish revival) for 44 years. To many Jewish people he was a living symbol of hope. The Rebbe, as he was affectionately known, became the embodiment of the hopes and dreams and aspirations of thousands.

The Rebbe of Brooklyn, New York, died at age 92 in June 1995. At his funeral, some of his followers celebrated and awaited his resurrection. But his grave remained silent. The devotion of his disciples was so deep that the loss of the Rebbe left them feeling profoundly distraught. One grieving follower wrote a tribute to the teacher who had given his life meaning and hope. In it he lamented, "I will miss the Rebbe for all of my days, but

> "Where is my Rebbe, and why have You taken him away? We are all so impoverished without him."

I shall not for a moment forget him. And I shall long to be reunited with him with the coming of the Messiah. Until then, I shall look to the heavens every morning, peering deep into the soul of the Creator, and ask, 'Where is my Rebbe, and why have You taken him away? We are all so impoverished without him.'"

Thousands of e-mailed and faxed prayers are brought daily to the Rebbe's grave in Brooklyn. Every day hundreds visit the cemetery. One of the graveside hosts said of these people, "They don't understand why they come. They're looking for direction, for a way to channel their spiritual reawakening to service for God."

The emotions of the widow and of Rebbe's followers must be similar to the emotions experienced at the death of Jesus Christ. The disillusioned followers of the Teacher from Nazareth had staked everything on Him. They had left their professions, their families, and their sins to follow Him. They had given up their own independence to rely on Him for every need of their life. He had given them hope, inspiration, and a sense of eternal dignity.

Yes, Jesus died and was buried. But then, like no other spiritual leader who has ever lived, He rose to assure His disciples that even though He was leaving, He was not leaving them abandoned and alone. Before leaving, He gave them a promise.

THE PROMISE OF THE SPIRIT

Two vivid images come to mind when I think of promises. One is the picture of Joe Namath sitting poolside in Miami prior to the 1969 Super Bowl and promising (actually guaranteeing!) that the upstart New York Jets would defeat the mighty Baltimore Colts—a promise he kept several days later to the shock of the sporting world.

The other image is of an incident that occurred a few years ago as I sat in a meeting with the president of the Baptist Union of Russia. He said that in the last few years, hundreds of Christian leaders had come from the West offering promises of help (both spiritual and financial), and that only one percent of those leaders had kept their promise.

The simple reality is that a promise is only as good as the willingness and ability of the one making it. What a comfort to know that when the Lord Jesus Christ makes a promise, He not only has the willingness to make the promise but also the eternal integrity and ability to keep it.

A promise is only as good as the willingness and ability of the one making it.

Of the many profound and significant promises our Lord made during His life on earth, few have more day-to-day potential for impact on us than His promise of the Spirit.

In His final words to the disciples before His crucifixion (Jn. 13–16), Jesus made a dramatic announcement of His soon departure. He was about to leave these friends with whom He had invested 3 years of His life. His words shocked and disturbed them. But He did not leave them without comfort. In response to their apprehension, He gave them a promise. He said, in effect, "Although I'm going away, the Holy Spirit is coming to minister to you in My place." It was a promise that unfolded in layers that began with what sounded more like a threat than a promise!

A SURPRISING DEPARTURE
"I go to My Father" (Jn. 14:12).

To the puzzlement of His disciples, Jesus had earlier spoken of going away (13:33,36). The fact that they could not follow was troubling to them. Later they would understand what He was sparing them from. For now, His words bewildered them.

Then He said it again (14:1-3). He told them He was going to the Father to prepare a place for them. It was becoming clear. He *was* going away. It was the fulfillment of His mission. How His heart must have ached for these dear friends, who were troubled and confused because they felt He was abandoning them!

The Big Picture
What Peter and company failed to see, of course, was the larger picture of the work of Christ. And no wonder. For 3 years they had been together. The group had shared experiences that went beyond their ability to fully understand or describe. Much of the significance of these events would not be clear to them until after the resurrection. John 12:16 tells us, "His disciples did

not understand these things at first; but when Jesus was glorified, then they remembered that these things were written about Him."

But with miracles still in their memory and with the thunderous shouts of the "Palm Sunday" crowd still ringing in their ears, all they could see was the moment. All they could do was stare at the One who, at His greatest moment of recognition, seemed determined to walk away from it all.

The Divine Mission

Jesus alone could see beyond the agony of the next few hours. He alone could see why it was so important for Him to die and then to return to the right hand of the Father (Mt. 26:64). There are a number of reasons why the Lord Jesus had to return to the Father:

- He had to return to the Father to be our great Mediator and Advocate (1 Tim. 2:5; 1 Jn. 2:1).
- He had to return to the Father so that He could prepare the eternal home He has promised us (Jn. 14:2).
- He had to go to the Father so that He might enter the heavenly sanctuary and be our Great High Priest (Heb. 6:19-20).
- He had to go to the Father to receive the glory due Him as the obedient, victorious Son (Jn. 17:24).
- He had to go to the Father so that He could gloriously return to establish the kingdom (Mt. 26:64).

When Jesus said He must go to the Father, it was not just a matter of a change of location—it was a change of operation. The plan of the Godhead for our redemption, and for the glory of God, was never *less* than the work of Christ on the cross—but it was eternally *more*.

A SERIOUS REQUEST
"I will pray the Father . . . " (Jn. 14:16).

The wonderful priestly ministry of Christ was promised as He prayed to the Father on behalf of His own. This is not something to take lightly. Such intercession is what He is now doing for us. As He prayed for His disciples, He is now praying for all those who are His.

Christ As Our Priest

The book of Hebrews has often been called the "Fifth Gospel" because it describes not only the past earthly ministry of Christ but the present heavenly one in which He acts as our Priest. The role of a priest in the Old Testament was to serve as the representative of man to God—and that is exactly what Jesus is doing for His own. He perpetually represents us before the Father in His ongoing work of ministry. The writer of Hebrews said:

He is also able to save to the uttermost those who come to God through Him, since He always lives to make intercession for them (Heb. 7:25).

When Jesus said, "I will pray the Father" (Jn. 14:16), it was the first hint of this priestly ministry for us. Although He was implicitly speaking of His intercessory ministry as Priest, He was explicitly speaking of one request in particular—and what a request it was! He must go to the Father specifically to request the dispatch of the Holy Spirit into the lives of believers.

The Holy Spirit's New Work

The sending of the Spirit would mark a powerful juncture in the dealings of God with man. Although the Holy Spirit had been active throughout history (Gen. 1:2; Ex. 31:3; 1 Sam. 19:23; 2 Chr. 24:20; Mt. 1:18; 12:28), He was about to do a new work in and among all who would be baptized into the body of Christ.

In the Old Testament, God the Father is portrayed as the member of the Godhead who plans and provides for His family on earth. In the incarnation, Christ is portrayed as the Son of the Father who comes to our rescue. Now, the Holy Spirit was about to become the One who would bring the life of the Godhead to those whom the Son brings to the Father.

How Does The Work Of The Spirit Fit Into The Eternal Plan?

The day of the Spirit is very significant. It shows a transition in the work of the Godhead, as the Triune God continues to unfold the divine plan. Later, we will more fully explore the purposes for the coming of the Holy Spirit. For now, it's important to recognize that each member of the Trinity, working together in perfect union, carries out a distinct role for the accomplishment of the eternal plan.

In this eternal plan, God the Father decreed the creation of man, decreed to allow sin (not cause it), and decreed that only by a perfect sacrifice could the penalty of sin be avoided.

In the eternal plan, God the Son is the Creator (Gen. 1; Jn. 1:1-3), the source of His people's provision, and ultimately the perfect sacrifice for sin. He became our Redeemer by becoming a man and sacrificially dying in our place.

In the same eternal plan, it became the role of the Spirit to apply that rescue to the lives of all who would believe in the Son. First, the Spirit would provide the divine strength that would enable the Son to be our example and Savior. Then, when the Son returned to the Father, the Spirit would begin baptizing people of all nations into the body of Christ on earth. Once Christ returned to the Father, the Spirit would come in His place to bring to completion God's wonderful plan for all who would receive forgiveness and new life in Christ Jesus.

Jesus' promise of the Spirit is all wrapped up in His declaration that He would "pray the Father." It is the opening of a new chapter in the dealings of God with mankind, in which the Holy Spirit is profoundly at work in people of all nations for the glory of the Son and to the worship of the Father.

A POWERFUL CONFIDENCE
". . . He will give you . . ." (Jn. 14:16).

This is the promise fulfilled. Notice again the relationship in the Godhead. Although absolutely equal to the Father, the Son submits to Him a request for His will to be done. The same is true of the Holy Spirit who, though absolutely equal to the Father, is sent forth by the Father to accomplish the Father's will. This is the wonder of the Trinity—one God manifesting Himself in three equal Persons who have varying roles for the purpose of accomplishing the eternal plan of God. The Son makes the request and the Spirit is dispatched, but it is the Father who gives the Spirit to men and women.

Confidence In Relationship
Notice the confidence of Christ's statement, "He will give you." It shows that He *knows* the answer will be given. It shows the confidence of the Son in the eternal plan that is yet unfolding. It shows His assurance in the ability of the Spirit to care for His children.

Confidence In The Divine Plan
As confident as Christ was of His impending death (Jn. 13:21), He was equally confident that the Father who decreed the cross to redeem a people for Himself would send the Spirit to care for those redeemed people. It was confidence in the eternal plan of the Father that enabled the Son to be willing to entrust those He had purchased with His own blood to the care and presence of the Spirit.

Confidence In The Need Of The World
The promise of the Spirit is for Christ's sake. It is for the care of those who are His. And it is for the sake of the whole world as well. In John 16, Jesus made it clear that when the Spirit came, He would not only work in the hearts of believers but also on the hearts of those

who do not yet know Christ. Jesus described the work of the Spirit in calling men and women to redemption when He said:

When He has come, He will convict the world of sin, and of righteousness, and of judgment: of sin, because they do not believe in Me; of righteousness, because I go to My Father and you see Me no more; of judgment, because the ruler of this world is judged (Jn. 16:8-11).

The Spirit would have a scope of ministry larger than just to those in the family of God. The Holy Spirit, grieved by sin, would seek the rescue of lost sinners and cause them to be conscious of their need of eternal life.

THE PERSON OF THE SPIRIT

We live in a culture that puts a high value on what is genuine. The largest selling soft drink company in the world refers to its product as "the real thing." And people are continually urged to "get real" by a sports clothing manufacturer. We are told to accept no substitutes, beware of cheap imitations, and check the label to assure ourselves that we are getting the "genuine article."

This is true even in other parts of the world. When shopping at the huge outdoor Moscow flea market in Ismailova Park, I saw at least five different kiosks displaying what were described as "handmade dolls," bearing the personal label of the woman who made them in her home. At each of these stands, the label said "Handmade by Tatiana." And each man who was selling the dolls said that Tatiana was his own wife. In fact, one of the kiosks was operated by a woman claiming to be the actual Tatiana!

None of us want to be left with less than we think we are given. Being shortchanged is something we fear. I wonder if such fears could have entered the minds of the disciples when Jesus said He was going away and sending a substitute. I wonder if they were fearful of getting less than what they had with Christ—some kind of a "cheap imitation."

Genuine Article Or Cheap Imitation?

If there were any such fears in the minds of the Master's men as they listened to the upper-room discourse, those concerns were addressed by Christ Himself. Even if the disciples could not yet understand, their fears would be answered by the precise terminology our Lord used to describe the divine Substitute He would send in His place. As Jesus described the Person of the Holy Spirit, His words made it abundantly clear that His disciples would not get less of God than they had with Him. They would receive a full inner presence of the Lord Jesus who would not only be *with* them, but would be *in* them.

Our Lord's choice of words as He spoke to the disciples is most critical. Let's look at the passage and the significant terms that tell the story:

> *I will pray the Father, and He will give you another Helper,*
> *that He may abide with you forever—the Spirit of truth,*
> *whom the world cannot receive, because it neither sees Him nor*
> *knows Him; but you know Him, for He dwells with you and*
> *will be in you (Jn. 14:16-17).*

The significant terms in these verses deserve careful consideration if we are to understand the full impact of the Lord's words.

"ANOTHER"

As a rule, some words and parts of speech give greater weight to the meaning of a text. For that reason, we almost always focus on nouns and verbs. Verbs relate the action of a statement, and nouns give and receive that action. So it is interesting when another part of speech takes a dominant role in how we understand a passage of Scripture. Such is the case here, where we turn to the adjective *another* to give clarity to the text.

When Is "Another" Not Another?

The word *another* is found 233 times in the New Testament, but it is not always the same Greek word. Along with several less significant terms, there are two primary Greek words that are translated *another*. One of these words is *heteros*, which means "another of a different kind." From it, we get words like *heterosexual* (relating to a different sex), *heterogeneous* (containing dissimilar parts), and *heterodox* (describing a different doctrinal message that is not orthodox).

Heteros is used, for example, in Acts 13:35 to speak of "another Psalm" (different from the one just referred to), and in Acts 17:7 it is used to distinguish "another king" (Christ, as set apart and different from Caesar). In each instance, it is clearly describing that which is distinctive and different from what it is compared to.

When Is "Another" Another?

In John 14:16, however, *heteros* is not the word Jesus used to describe the promise of the Spirit. To describe the Holy Spirit, our Lord used the word *allos*, which means just the opposite of *heteros*. *Allos* means "another of the same kind." When Jesus used this term, He was making a bold promise that the Comforter He would send would be a perfect Substitute. In His co-equal, co-eternal nature, the Holy Spirit would be *another* just like Jesus Himself.

Allos is the word used in the "one another" statements of the New Testament that challenge and encourage us to befriend other believers—those who are just like ourselves in our imperfect flesh and in our relationship to Christ. The trouble with us is that even though we are like one another in sharing the same imperfect flesh, we don't like to admit it. We often disagree with, disregard, and condemn those who are just like ourselves. This is not true of the Spirit's relationship to the Son and the Father. The members of the Trinity are always in perfect harmony with one another.

The Holy Spirit is always in step with the desires and affections that Christ has for us. The Spirit cares for us with the same love, the same concern, the same grace, the same compassion, the same truth, the same justice, the same holiness, and the same power that the disciples saw in the Lord Jesus Christ's ministry during the 3 years He shared with them.

"COMFORTER"

Not all of our understanding of the Spirit comes from the word *another*. We must also give consideration to the word it modifies—*Comforter*. Another of like kind besides Jesus is wonderful—but another what? Here our Lord used *parakaleo*, a very descriptive word that would have been familiar to the disciples. It was used in a variety of ways in the culture of the day. *Smith's Bible Dictionary* tells us that this word was used to describe a legal assistant, advocate, or one who pleads another's cause. This describes the Person and work of the Holy Spirit, who becomes our Paraclete and Advocate with the Father—like Jesus, our Great High Priest and Mediator.

How Many Comforters Do I Need?

When John's Gospel is compared with his New Testament letters, it becomes apparent that he dealt in some detail with the idea of dual Paracletes. He discussed the role of the Holy Spirit as our Comforter here in John 14, and the role of Christ as our Advocate in 1 John 2:1. In that passage he wrote, "My little children, these things I write to you, so that you may not sin. And if anyone sins, we have an Advocate with the Father, Jesus Christ the righteous."

Why two divine Paracletes? Greek scholar and New Testament commentator A. T. Robertson describes the difference of their function this way: "So the Christian has Christ as his Paraclete with the Father, the Holy Spirit as the Father's Paraclete with us (Jn. 14:16,26; 15:26; 16:7; 1 Jn. 2:1)."

What Will These Comforters Do?

How does this work and what does it accomplish? Perhaps it is best to see these two ministries of advocacy as similar but accomplishing very different goals.

The Role Of Christ. As our Advocate, Christ defends us before the Father to keep us secure. It is a part of His promise that "the one who comes to Me I will by no means cast out" (Jn. 6:37). What a rich promise! Christ Himself serves as our Defender. He doesn't defend our works, which are flawed and faulty. His defense of us is based on His perfect and completed work.

The Role Of The Spirit. The Holy Spirit as our Comforter works within us to declare to us the abiding presence of the living God in our lives. Romans 8 talks extensively about this wonderful work of the Spirit. Paul wrote, "As many as are led by the Spirit of God, these are sons of God. For you did not receive the spirit of bondage again to fear, but you received the Spirit of adoption by whom we cry out, 'Abba, Father.' The Spirit Himself bears witness with our spirit that we are children of God" (vv.14-16). The role of the Spirit as our Comforter, in part, is to assure us of the wonderful position that is ours as the children of the living God!

"THE SPIRIT OF TRUTH"

This final phrase that our Lord used to describe the promise of the Spirit has significant implications all its own. Jesus used it in John 14:17 to show another facet of the Spirit's ministry. At the same time, He gave definition to the Holy Spirit's character. Just moments before, Jesus had told His men that He alone was the way, the truth, and the life (14:6). Now He tells them specifically how the Spirit is "another of the exact same kind" by referring to Him as the "Spirit of truth."

A. T. Robertson has an interesting note on the title "the Spirit of truth." He says that it is appropriate because "the Holy Spirit is marked by it [truth], gives it, defends it, [and is] in contrast to the spirit of error."

Integrity

The Spirit is *marked by truth* because of His divine nature. As God He has all the attributes of deity, one of which is truth. He does not have the capacity to lie and is therefore absolutely trustworthy in all He says.

In this truthfulness of the Spirit, it is apparent why those who want to be in step with the Spirit must long to be people of integrity. We cannot hope to be under His influence if we are consciously distorting the truth in a misguided effort to protect ourselves or someone else.

Inspiration

The Spirit *gives truth* in the sense of divine inspiration (2 Pet. 1:21). He is the dispenser of all biblical truth. The Word of God is reliable because it came to us under the guidance of the Spirit of truth.

Invincibility

The Spirit *defends the truth* by empowering the preaching and teaching of the Word of God, which proclaims the truth and answers the arguments of the world against it. In the ministry of proclamation, the Word of God is not only announced but exonerated.

Incompatibility

The Holy Spirit of truth *stands in stark contrast* to our spiritual enemy. Satan, a mere created, fallen being, is the father of lies (Jn. 8:44). Satan is in the business of deception and subtle trickery (Gen. 3; 2 Cor. 11:3,14). The Holy Spirit deals in the truth. In fact, this is a large part of what He was sent into the world to do. As we saw earlier, the Spirit was sent to expose the truth to a lost world by convicting the world of sin and righteousness and judgment (Jn. 16:8)—a hard but eternally necessary truth about the world's condition.

Occasionally in major dramatic plays and musicals, the star of the show (the lead) becomes ill, needs time away for another project, or will be gone for some reason. In those times, a substitute steps into the lead role (a stand-in). When that happens and the stand-in is announced, there is generally a groan from the crowd. The stand-in will do his or her best, and may actually do a better job than the star, but it is still a disappointment to the audience.

It should be a great comfort to us that Jesus did not send an inferior stand-in or second-best. Our Savior sent in His place a co-equal, co-eternal member of the Trinity. He would perfectly represent Christ and the Father in the lives of God's beloved children.

There can be no question about the divine nature of the Holy Spirit, and there can be no question about His perfect character. He is our Comforter, another of the exact same kind as Jesus, who gives and substantiates the truth.

THE PRESENCE OF THE SPIRIT

Ebenezer Scrooge is the notorious main character of Charles Dickens' classic, "A Christmas Carol." It is the story of one man's struggle to develop a heart for people. Behind all the action and teaching, however, are the three spirits (the ghosts of Christmas past, present, and future) who maneuver Scrooge to his various destinations.

It is interesting to note the character of these spirits as they come and go, move in and out, appear and then just as quickly disappear. If we were truly dependent on such flighty characters for wisdom and direction and guidance and instruction, our lives would have the stability of jello.

By contrast, we have from Jesus the promise of a Spirit who abides with us consistently, allowing us to live dependently on Him with great confidence. Notice how different the Holy Spirit is from Dickens' Christmas spirits.

A PERMANENT HELPER
". . . abide with you forever" (Jn. 14:16).
By this statement, Jesus assured us of a New Covenant relationship to the Spirit. This relationship was both alike and different from the way the Holy Spirit had related to the people of God in earlier times.

The Way It Used To Be
In the Old Testament, the Holy Spirit was active in a variety of ways. He was active in creation (Gen. 1:2; Job 33:4), in conviction (Gen. 6:3), in confirmation of the

Word of God (2 Chr. 24:20), and in caring for the people of God (Ps. 51:12). This was all accomplished by the Spirit as the agent of the Father, the One who is given primary emphasis in the Old Testament era.

In the Old Testament, the Holy Spirit was involved in empowering people for acts of service, which is similar to His role today. In Old Testament times, any good or honorable act had to be energized by the Spirit and grace of God. Man, in his fallen nature, has always been unable to do anything that would please God. But it is also true that in the Old Testament the Holy Spirit came upon the Lord's people as they needed Him or as He sovereignly chose to use them (as with Samson).

Throughout Old Testament history, the Spirit would come upon people for seasons of ministry and empower them for acts of skill, strength, or insight. The Spirit of God was described as coming upon them (see the messengers of Saul in 1 Sam. 19:20 and Gideon in Jud. 6:34), and then would depart (see the 70 elders of Israel in Num. 11:25).

Sometimes the Spirit's departure would occur because of sin. This was certainly the concern of David as he mourned the sin he had committed with Bathsheba. He prayed, "Do not cast me away from Your presence, and do not take Your Holy Spirit from me" (Ps. 51:11). David's fear seems to have been that the Holy Spirit might leave him because of his sin.

Sometimes the Spirit was said to depart because the task for which someone had been empowered was accomplished (Num. 11:25). This was apparently the case with several of the minor prophets, who were boldly empowered by the Spirit for very brief prophetic ministries and then went back to whatever their life had been previously. It most certainly was the case with Amos, a shepherd from Tekoa until he was called to speak prophetic words from God (the book of Amos).

The ministry of the Spirit was described differently in the Old Testament than it was in the New Testament. For this reason Christ's disciples, still living in the Old Testament era, would see the Lord's declaration of a permanent abiding of the Spirit as a great contrast to their previous understanding.

The Way It Is In Christ

The promised permanent presence of the Spirit in John 14:16 would also be in contrast to their mere 3-year physical relationship with Christ Himself. He did not come to dwell permanently on earth in a physical body. He came to accomplish the plan of redemption and then return to the Father's presence. The Spirit's coming would be very different from His ministry in the Old Testament and different from Christ's ministry in the Gospels, for His coming to indwell believers was promised to be eternal in nature.

A DISTINCTIVE PRESENCE

"... *whom the world cannot receive*" (*Jn.* 14:17).

This statement opens up an issue of enormous significance to the believer, for it sets us in contrast to an unredeemed world. In 1 Corinthians 2–3, we find the contrast of the natural man with the spiritual man:

Now we have received, not the spirit of the world, but the Spirit who is from God, that we might know the things that have been freely given to us by God. These things we also speak, not in words which man's wisdom teaches but which the Holy Spirit teaches, comparing spiritual things with spiritual. But the natural man does not receive the things of the Spirit of God, for they are foolishness to him; nor can he know them, because they are spiritually discerned. But he who is spiritual judges all things, yet he himself is rightly judged by no one. For "who has known the mind of the Lord that he may instruct Him?" But we have the mind of Christ (1 Cor. 2:12-16).

What The Spiritual Man Has

It couldn't be more clear. Children of God are different from the unbelievers. We have the presence of the Spirit of God in our lives, an unbeliever (the natural man) does not. We are enabled by the Spirit to know the things given to us by God (v.12), to understand spiritual things (v.13), to have spiritual discernment (v.15), and to have the mind of Christ (v.16). These rich blessings are not given to everyone who is born, only to those who are born of faith.

What The Natural Man Doesn't Have

The key to the contrast is in verse 14: "The natural man does not receive the things of the Spirit of God, for they are foolishness to him; nor can he know them, because they are spiritually discerned." The natural man cannot understand what it means to live for the honor of Christ because he is not of the same spirit. He can study the Bible as literature, but he cannot see the wonder of God in Christ. He hears spiritual principles, but he cannot apply them in the love and faith of Christ. Why? Because he does not have the Spirit of God.

Jesus said that the world cannot receive the Spirit. This is undeniably revealed in the contrast of what the Spirit of God produces and what the spirit of man (the world) produces. It is the difference between the wisdom that is from above and the wisdom that is of this world. James 3 delivers the contrast in clear-cut terms:

> Who is wise and understanding among you? Let him show by good conduct that his works are done in the meekness of wisdom. But if you have bitter envy and self-seeking in your hearts, do not boast and lie against the truth. This wisdom does not descend from above, but is earthly, sensual, demonic. For where envy and self-seeking exist, confusion and every evil thing are there. But the wisdom that is from above is first pure, then peaceable, gentle, willing to yield, full of mercy and good fruits, without partiality and without hypocrisy. Now the fruit of righteousness is sown in peace by those who make peace (vv. 13-18).

Although the Holy Spirit is not mentioned explicitly in James 3, it is obvious from 1 Corinthians 2–3 (as well as Acts 6:3,10 and Eph. 1:17) that spiritual wisdom (James calls it "wisdom from above") is imparted by the Holy Spirit and is very different from the wisdom displayed by the natural man, who does not receive the Spirit.

A RESIDENT WITHIN

"He dwells with you and will be in you" (Jn. 14:17).
This is the final declaration of the significant way the Spirit's presence is displayed in our lives. It is not only a matter of an eternal presence, or even a presence that

displays itself in true spiritual wisdom. It is the amazing reality of the Spirit of the living God taking up personal residence *in* the lives of believers. Two great realities flow from this wonderful truth:

The Indwelling Of The Spirit

Jesus introduced the subject here, and did so by setting it in contrast to the work of the Spirit in the Old Testament. The contrast is between "dwells *with* you" and "will be *in* you." This proclaims that the promise of the Holy Spirit is not coming in some general way to the world, but specifically into the lives of believers. Paul echoed that same theme in Romans 8 in relation to our understanding of the Holy Spirit. Notice how clearly he described the indwelling of the Spirit in verses 9-11:

> *You are not in the flesh but in the Spirit, if indeed the Spirit of God dwells in you. Now if anyone does not have the Spirit of Christ, he is not His. And if Christ is in you, the body is dead because of sin, but the Spirit is life because of righteousness. But if the Spirit of Him who raised Jesus from the dead dwells in you, He who raised Christ from the dead will also give life to your mortal bodies through His Spirit who dwells in you.*

The Spirit has come to indwell us as the ultimate evidence that we have received eternal life through the resurrected Christ. To not have the Spirit is to not have Christ. To know Christ is to enjoy the blessing of the indwelling Holy Spirit.

The Filling Of The Spirit

This is very different from the indwelling of the Spirit, but it flows from it. The filling of the Spirit (Eph. 5:18) speaks of His control and influence in our lives. As the influence of alcohol has control over people for evil, so the Spirit's presence has influence and control over believers for good when we surrender our will to Him.

If the Spirit were not indwelling us, He could not continually fill us with His controlling power. Although indwelling is permanent and filling must be maintained moment-by-moment, they are still connected by the reality of the presence of the Holy Spirit in our lives.

The Point Of His Presence

What's the implication? It is stated boldly by Paul in 1 Corinthians 6:19-20.

Do you not know that your body is the temple of the Holy Spirit who is in you, whom you have from God, and you are not your own? For you were bought at a price; therefore glorify God in your body and in your spirit, which are God's.

The presence of the Holy Spirit should result in clearly seen holiness, for we are now His temple, where He abides continually—even forever. It is not just the empowering we need to glorify God, it is our motivation as well.

The Holy Spirit lives within us. His presence is evidence of the price Christ paid to redeem us from the consequence of sin and secure us for all eternity. We are not our own. We have been bought with a price. Now we have the Spirit of God indwelling us.

We must give the Spirit control over our lives for Him to do His work in us, for we desperately need Him. The work that He lives in us to do is the work we could never do for ourselves. It is divine enablement that comes by the will of the Father, to the honor of the Son, by the immediate and direct empowering of the Spirit. It is work that we can prayerfully ask for, inviting Him daily, hourly, and even minute by minute to have His wonderful way in our lives.

THE POWER OF THE SPIRIT

The first winter that my wife Marlene and I were married was marked by severe blizzards. I can vividly remember one Sunday when we awoke to find that the electricity had been knocked out by an ice storm. Huddled around a battery-powered radio for news on that frigid Sunday, we heard a most unusual announcement. The announcer, before giving the list of church services canceled due to the ice storm, said, "The following churches will be closed due to lack of power." What an interesting comment! I knew what he meant, but I was struck by what he said.

The idea of churches closing due to lack of power conjures up some spiritual parallels that directly tie into Jesus' promise of the Spirit. Just prior to His ascension, Jesus told His men in Acts 1:8, "You shall receive power when the Holy Spirit has come upon you; and you shall be witnesses to Me in Jerusalem, and in all Judea and Samaria, and to the end of the earth." He directly attached the coming of the Spirit to the empowering of believers. This gives us reason to examine some important issues in this concluding section of "The Promise Of The Spirit."

What Is Power?

The word *power* used by Jesus in Acts 1:8 is the Greek word *dunamis*. It is defined variously as "strength, power, or ability." Specifically, it refers to "inherent power, power residing in a thing by virtue of its nature, or which a person or thing exerts and puts forth." This spiritual power is not inherent to the believer, however. Notice very carefully that it is inherent to the Person of the Holy Spirit who resides within the believer. How does this power manifest itself in our lives? I would suggest that there are at least three (though probably more) clear ways the Holy Spirit expresses His power in the lives of the redeemed.

Power For Life. How does the Spirit express life in us? By causing our lives to be profoundly different from the hopeless world that surrounds us. Notice Paul's words in Romans 15:13, "Now may the God of hope fill you with all joy and peace in believing, that you may abound in hope by the power of the Holy Spirit."

The power of the Holy Spirit provides for us the things that human effort and human religion and human righteousness could never achieve. He is there to empower our living with a glorious sense of joy, peace, and hope that can carry us through the trials and hardships that are the inevitable by-products of life in a fallen world.

The power we need is found in a Person who has been sent by the Father to bring fullness to our lives.

The power we need is found in a Person who has been sent by the Father to bring fullness to our lives.

In a world that is in mad pursuit of happiness, we can have joy by the power of the Holy Spirit. In a world that is crying out from the grief of constant conflict, we can have true peace. In a world that is filled with empty despair and a bleak future, we can have a bright hope. Why? Because the power of the Holy Spirit can equip us for life in a way that the world cannot grasp. His power can enable us to experience the things that the world craves and cannot secure, but are ours by the Spirit. This is the abundant life Jesus spoke of—a life that is full and rich and deep and lasting. A life that is lived by the power of the Holy Spirit. The hymnwriter Thomas Chisholm expressed the joy of this when he wrote:

Pardon for sin
and a peace that endureth,
Thine own dear presence
to cheer and to guide;
Strength for today
and bright hope for tomorrow—
Blessings all mine,
with ten thousand beside!
Great is Thy faithfulness!

©Renewal 1951, Hope Publishing Co.

Power For Outreach. This, of course, is specifically what is in view in Acts 1:8. But the power of the Holy Spirit in evangelism and missions is not limited to that text. Notice two great statements by Paul on this subject:

My speech and my preaching were not with persuasive words of human wisdom, but in demonstration of the Spirit and of power (1 Cor. 2:4).

Our gospel did not come to you in word only, but also in power, and in the Holy Spirit and in much assurance, as you know what kind of men we were among you for your sake (1 Th. 1:5).

In both of these texts, Paul was writing to churches he had established. He made it clear, however, that it was not by his wisdom or cleverness or ability to craft words. It was only by the Holy Spirit that they had been brought to saving faith.

> *Only by the power of the Spirit can true evangelism be accomplished.*

In a day of cleverly packaged, methodically dominated, and man-centered evangelism, it is refreshing to be reminded that only by the power of the Spirit can true evangelism be accomplished and the mission of the church to reach the world with the gospel be performed.

Power For Ministry In The Church. True ministry within the body of Christ is not achieved by human brilliance or skill but by the work of the Holy Spirit. The Spirit gives special abilities (spiritual gifts) to believers "for the equipping of the saints for the work of ministry, for the edifying of the body of Christ" (Eph. 4:12; cp. 1 Cor. 14:26; 1 Th. 5:11).

What Are The "Greater Works" That Jesus Promised In John 14:12?

Notice the words of Christ, "Most assuredly, I say to you, he who believes in Me, the works that I do he will do also; and greater works than these he will do, because I go to My Father." The problem is that this verse has been used to validate all kinds of activities today by calling them "greater works." The question that must be carefully examined is how should the word *greater* be defined? Greater in power? Greater in scope? Greater in effectiveness? What are "greater works"?

Is it reasonable to think that we will be enabled to accomplish works of greater power or quality than Jesus did? Think of the nature of His miracles—feeding the multitudes, raising the dead, healing the incurable, controlling the forces of nature by the power of His word. Now consider why He did these things. John 20:30-31 gives us the motive behind the miracles.

Truly Jesus did many other signs in the presence of His disciples, which are not written in this book; but these are written that you may believe that Jesus is the Christ, the Son of God, and that believing you may have life in His name.

The purpose of the wondrous things that Jesus did was to reveal the uniqueness of His Person as the Son of God. Certainly we do not seek to accomplish such a goal, for we do not have the right to make such a claim.

No, we are not to do works greater in quality or power, for He alone is Christ. What then are the "greater works"? The best understanding of it, and one commonly held by many respected Bible teachers, is that the phrase speaks not of the *quality* of the works but of the *scope* of the works. Think about it.

Such an expectation [greater works] seems impossible in the light of His character and power; yet, through the power of the Spirit whom Jesus sent after His ascension, there were more converts after the initial sermon of Peter at Pentecost than recorded for Jesus during His entire career. The influence of the infant church covered the Roman world, whereas Jesus during His lifetime never traveled outside the boundaries of Palestine. Through the disciples He multiplied His ministry after His departure. The book of Acts is a continuous record of deeds that followed the precedent that Jesus had begun. As the living Lord He continued in His church what He had Himself begun. He expected that the church would become the instrument by which He could manifest Himself to all people (Merrill C. Tenney, *Expositor's Bible Commentary*, Zondervan Publishing House, ©1981, Vol.9, pp.145-146).

We should be humbled by the glorious promise that by the power of the Spirit we can be used of God to perform His work on a broad scale—even to the ends of the earth.

What Are The Implications?

Perhaps the verse that captures the implications of these truths is 2 Corinthians 3:18, "We all, with unveiled face, beholding as in a mirror the glory of the Lord, are being transformed into the same image from glory to glory, just as by the Spirit of the Lord." It is by the work of the Holy Spirit that spiritual transformation takes place. This involves every area of our spiritual lives.

Spiritual Growth. It is the Spirit that matures us into the image of Christ so that we can give glory to the Lord Jesus Christ (Gal. 3:1-5). We are called to be submissive to His control in our lives. That is our responsibility. But the Holy Spirit is the One who produces the image and likeness of Christ in us.

> *The Holy Spirit is the One who produces the image and likeness of Christ in us.*

Spiritual Gifts. We are personally enabled by the Spirit to perform various kinds of spiritual ministry (see 1 Cor. 12; Rom. 12; Eph. 4:7-16; 1 Pet. 4:10-11). It is not by our own seeking or determination (1 Cor. 12:11). Notice that spiritual gifts are not given for personal edification or glory. These gifts are given for ministry to the body of Christ, the church (1 Cor. 12:7). They are not to be exercised in pride, but in spiritual humility (Rom. 12:3). Spiritual gifts have not been given so that we all fall in step with a common experience. Because of diversity in the body of Christ (1 Cor. 12:4-6), its many unique and varied members can contribute to the building up of the body (Rom. 12:4-8). It is helpful to be reminded that spiritual gifts are tools to be worked with, not toys to be played with. They are the instruments by which we perform our spiritual service, bearing fruit to the glory of the Father.

Spiritual Worship. It is by the Spirit that we are able to give true worship to the living God (Jn. 4:24). This worship, however, is always protected by the authority and guidelines of the Word of God. This is stated directly in John 4 and reinforced in the guidelines for gifts in worship in 1 Corinthians 12 and 14.

Jesus called His disciples to glorify the Father by bearing much fruit (Jn. 15:8). At the same time, the

Lord made it clear: "Without Me you can do nothing" (Jn. 15:5). How can these two directives be resolved when He had just said that He was going away? Jesus resolved them in the promise of the Holy Spirit.

It is Jesus' desire that we glorify the Father, so He gave to His followers the indwelling Holy Spirit to make it possible. How tragic that so often we live life totally oblivious to this wonderful Comforter in our lives! We often ignore His enabling by which we give glory to God in our spiritual growth, in our worship, and in our service to Him.

We live in a society that truly needs to see the glory of God expressed in a spiritually mature and empowered church. May we submit to the ministry of the One who has come to magnify God in Christ and see His great work among the people of God. Let's pray with Paul, "To Him be glory in the church by Christ Jesus to all generations, forever and ever. Amen" (Eph. 3:21).

LIVING IN THE SPIRIT

To experience Jesus' promise of the Spirit, two foundational truths must be acknowledged. The first is that those who are in Christ must submit to the Spirit if they are going to grow in Christlikeness. Galatians 3:3 asks, "Are you so foolish? Having begun in the Spirit, are you now being made perfect by the flesh?" As the work of the Holy Spirit is a necessary part of our salvation, His work is also vital to our Christian living.

In this light, will you as a believer give careful thought to the extent to which you consciously submit to the control of the Spirit and allow Him to guide your life? Will you consider what kind of temple you are providing for His dwelling place? Will you acknowledge that He is the *Holy* Spirit, and allow Him to produce godliness in your life? This is essential to living the Christian life. And as we experience this wonderful reality, we can know the joy of Christ and intimacy of fellowship with Him.

If you don't yet know Jesus Christ as your Savior and Lord, your need is different. You are still in your sins and apart from the Spirit of God. But you don't need to stay there. You can find hope in the simple but profound truth that Christ died for your sins and will bring those who believe in Him to the Father.

> *His cross provides forgiveness, and His Spirit offers His presence.*

He is the Savior who gave Himself in sacrifice for your sin. And He gave His Spirit for your comfort and strength. His cross provides forgiveness, and His Spirit offers His presence. Accept Christ by faith as your Savior, and allow the Spirit of God to begin His wonderful work in your life today!

TWO

HOW CAN I BE FILLED WITH THE HOLY SPIRIT?

And just exactly what does that mean? If I am filled with the Spirit, will I know it? These questions are being asked today by Christians who want to walk with God and please Him. Yet some are afraid they are missing out when they hear about others who claim to have had a special filling of the Spirit.

RBC senior research editor Herb Vander Lugt has examined what the Bible has to say about this subject. We pray that this chapter will help many to have a deeper understanding and experience of the Spirit-filled life.

Martin R. De Haan II

What Some People Are Saying

Every follower of Jesus Christ should want to obey the biblical command to be filled with the Holy Spirit. But what does that involve? Some see it as an experience that is recognized by:

- speaking in "tongues"
- feelings of wild ecstasy
- feeling the Spirit take them over
- being overcome with great joy
- being "slain" in the Spirit
- having the ability to prophesy
- being able to interpret "tongues"

But other Christians say they have never had any of these experiences. They claim that a person does not have to have any of these things happen to him to show that he is filled with the Holy Spirit. They believe that a Christian can be filled with the Holy Spirit as he lives his day-to-day life.

To them, Richard Wurmbrand, who still carries scars from beatings he received in a communist prison camp, exemplifies the power of a Spirit-filled life. He tells of singing for joy in a cell where he was cold, sick, and hungry. To many, he is a good example of someone who is Spirit-filled.

A Christian named John, who died in a Grand Rapids nursing home a few years ago, was considered a Spirit-filled man by those who took care of him. During the last 2 years of his life, as cancer ravaged his body, his joy was irrepressible. He told everybody he met about Jesus Christ.

During the first year, John asked the aids to wheel

him into rooms where people were discouraged and depressed. His testimony was used to lead many of his fellow residents to the Lord. After he could no longer be placed in a wheelchair, he talked to people who came into his room. He radiated such joy that they couldn't help but feel they were in the presence of a Spirit-filled man.

He radiated such joy that they couldn't help but feel they were in the presence of a Spirit-filled man.

According to the Bible, the privilege for every believer to be filled with the Holy Spirit began at Pentecost (Acts 2:1-13). The disciples were praying together when they suddenly heard the sound of rushing wind, saw tonguelike flames, and spoke in languages they had never learned. As a result, 3,000 people in Jerusalem trusted Christ that very day. The apostles were filled with courage and power, witnessing boldly and performing miracles. As time went on, and despite persecution, these Spirit-filled Christians presented such a powerful testimony that even their enemies spoke of them as men who had "turned the world upside down" (Acts 17:6).

We would all like to be filled with the Holy Spirit. But most of us don't experience the same victory, the same joy, or the same power as these early apostles. So, this leads us to ask, "How can I be filled with the Holy Spirit?"

WHO IS THE HOLY SPIRIT?

Before we can discuss being filled with the Holy Spirit, we need to know who the Holy Spirit is. Some people insist that the Holy Spirit is an influence—a power or source of God-given spiritual energy. Others see Him as a ghostlike force, entering or leaving us at will. Others picture Him as a kind of cosmic magician, elusive and vague, who drops mysteriously into our lives to make religious things happen and then leaves just as quickly as He came.

The Bible makes it clear, however, that the Holy Spirit is a person who lives within every Christian. It also teaches that He is God, the Third Person of the Trinity.

He Is A Person

The Scriptures give us five clear evidences that the Holy Spirit is a person, not just a mystic force or strange power.

1. **The Holy Spirit is spoken of as "He."** Jesus referred to the Holy Spirit as "He." He promised His disciples: "I will pray the Father, and He will give you another Helper, that He [the Holy Spirit] may abide with you forever" (Jn. 14:16).

2. **The Holy Spirit has intelligence.** He knows the "deep things of God" and reveals them to us (1 Cor. 2:10-11). Only a person has this kind of intelligence.

3. **The Holy Spirit makes decisions.** He gives gifts to the Lord's people, "distributing to each one individually as He wills"(1 Cor. 12:11). Only a personal being can make decisions.

4. **The Holy Spirit has emotions.** He feels love (Rom. 15:30) and grief (Eph. 4:30). An influence cannot feel emotions like these.
5. **The Holy Spirit is active.** He does things only a person can do:
   - speaks (Rev. 2:7)
   - intercedes (Rom. 8:26)
   - teaches (Jn. 14:26)
   - leads (Rom. 8:14)
   - appoints (Acts 20:28)
   - empowers (Acts 1:8)

He Is God

The Holy Spirit is also referred to in the Bible as God. He is the Third Person of the eternal Trinity, one with the Father and with the Son. The following factors show His deity:

1. **The Spirit's name appears as equal with the Father and the Son in the formula for baptism and in some of the New Testament prayers** (Mt. 28:19; 2 Cor. 13:14).
2. **The apostle Peter said that the Holy Spirit was God.** When Ananias' sin was exposed, Peter told him that he had lied to the Holy Spirit. He went on to say that this lie had not been "to men but to God" (Acts 5:3-4).
3. **The Holy Spirit is called "Lord"** (2 Cor. 3:17-18).
4. **The Holy Spirit possesses qualities that belong only to God:** eternality (Heb. 9:14), the ability to be everywhere at the same time (Ps. 139:7-10), sovereign power (Lk. 1:35,37), and the knowledge of "the things of God" (1 Cor. 2:10-12).

The Bible teaches that the Holy Spirit, who lives within every Christian, is a person and that He is God. Admittedly we can't grasp the great mystery of how the Holy Spirit can live within us. But we don't have to understand it. We just have to trust that what the Bible says is true.

WHO CAN BE FILLED WITH THE HOLY SPIRIT?

The filling of the Holy Spirit should be the desire of every Christian. But listening to how some people talk, one could get the idea that it is reserved only for privileged, spiritually sensitive, special people. We are convinced, however, that the filling of the Holy Spirit is for everyone. But there are two important prerequisites.

First, to experience the filling of the Holy Spirit a person must be a Christian—he must be born again. This new birth is given by the Holy Spirit. When Jesus told Nicodemus that he had to be born again, He referred to it as being "born of the Spirit" (Jn. 3:6). He later told His disciples, "It is the Spirit who gives life" (Jn. 6:63).

When the Spirit gives this new life, He also enters into the new Christian to live within him permanently—to indwell. Anyone who does not have the indwelling Holy Spirit is not a Christian (Rom. 8:9). Even though the indwelling of the Spirit is *not* the same thing as the filling of the Spirit, only someone who is indwelt can be filled. So, the first prerequisite to being Spirit-filled is to be a Christian.

Second, the filling of the Holy Spirit is only for those Christians who want to be filled. Although He dwells within all Christians, He does not fill them just because He is present. To be obedient to the command to be filled with the Spirit (Eph. 5:18), a person must want the Spirit's filling and then be willing to yield to His control.

WHAT IS THE FILLING OF THE HOLY SPIRIT?

Before we can answer the question "How can I be filled with the Holy Spirit?" we must know what the filling of the Spirit is. The filling of the Spirit is the influence or control the Holy Spirit exercises over us when we yield ourselves to Him. The Spirit of God, who has given us new life and who has taken up residence within us, wants to fill our lives with His goodness and power. He wants us to let Him take control of our lives. Even so, He does not use His power as God to overwhelm us; rather, He fills us only as we submit to Him.

In this sense, then, being filled with the Spirit means that we have placed ourselves under His influence and control. We have yielded to Him, letting Him take over our lives.

We often speak of something that so fills a person's mind that it strangely influences everything he thinks and does. For example, a person can be filled with:

- anger
- fear

- jealousy
- remorse
- sorrow
- pride
- love
- anxiety

The Bible itself uses the word *filled* in the same way (see Lk. 6:11; Acts 5:17; 13:45).

To be filled with something, therefore, means to be under its control. This truth is stated clearly regarding the Holy Spirit in Ephesians 5:18.

Do not be drunk with wine, in which is dissipation; but be filled with the Spirit.

Paul used this analogy because a person who becomes intoxicated with alcohol places himself under its influence or control. Similarly, a Christian who submits to the leading of the indwelling Holy Spirit puts himself under His influence or control. Both the person who consumes enough alcohol to become drunk and the Christian who yields to the Holy Spirit have placed

A person who is drunk with wine:	A person who is filled with the Spirit:
• walks different	• walks different
• talks different	• talks different
• acts different	• acts different
• thinks different	• thinks different
• feels different	• feels different
Alcohol's control results in impaired judgment.	The Spirit's control results in improved judgment.

themselves under the control of something or someone outside themselves.

On the Day of Pentecost, people who heard the apostles speak in languages they had never learned accused them of being drunk. Moreover, in the pagan ceremonies of Paul's day, worshipers often got drunk to have a "religious experience." The analogy, therefore, had some background in Paul's thinking. And if you stop to think about it, a group of Spirit-filled Christians singing with great enthusiasm may have a superficial resemblance to a band of pagan worshipers, drunk with wine, singing praises to their gods.

The similarity, as already indicated, is only on the surface. A person who is drunk with wine, and therefore under its control, suffers impaired judgment. He says and does things he normally wouldn't do, and he often can't remember what he did. On the other hand, a person filled with the Holy Spirit, and therefore under His control, enjoys improved judgment, acts in a sane and responsible manner, and rejoices in the memory of what he said and did while under the control of the Holy Spirit.

We are greatly influenced by whatever it is that "fills" us. If we are filled with anger, we will be influenced to such an extent that we will say and do things we may later regret. A person who is filled with anger against God may become so controlled by his hatred that he becomes irreverent, blasphemous, defiant, and rebellious toward everything.

To be filled with the Holy Spirit, then, is to be so influenced by, controlled by, or permeated by Him that we will reflect God's moral character and be strengthened by His power. We will be loving, joyful, peaceful, patient, kind, good, faithful, gentle, and self-controlled—virtues that Paul referred to as "the fruit of the Spirit" (Gal. 5:22-23).

HOW CAN I BE FILLED WITH THE HOLY SPIRIT?

Paul commanded the believers at Ephesus—and every Christian—to be "filled with the Spirit" (5:18). This clause could be literally translated, "Let the Holy Spirit keep filling you," or "Keep letting the Holy Spirit fill you."

But just how do we obey this command? What must we do to let the Holy Spirit keep filling us? How can we be filled with the Holy Spirit?

Well, we know what it means to be filled with excitement or happiness. Excitement or happiness so permeates our thoughts and feelings that it dominates us. When a young woman first becomes engaged, she is often so excited and happy that it influences everything she does.

When Paul told us to be filled with the Spirit, he was telling us to let Him so fill us that everything we think and do is influenced or controlled by Him.

But the crucial question is still, "How?" God's part is clear: He will fill us. But what is our part? Being filled with the Holy Spirit involves four essentials. We must: (1) be Christ-centered, (2) be in the Word, (3) be submissive, and (4) be confident.

We will now look in detail at each of these four essentials for being filled with the Holy Spirit.

ESSENTIAL ONE:
Be Christ-Centered

The first essential for being Spirit-filled is to center our lives on Jesus Christ. He must be the focal point of our thoughts and aspirations. In all we do, we must be conscious of following His example and doing His will. When we are Christ-centered, we are pleasing the Holy Spirit because that's what He wants us to do. In fact, Jesus said, "He [the Holy Spirit] will glorify Me, for He will take of what is Mine and declare it to you" (Jn. 16:14). In a good marriage, the wife or husband enjoys seeing the other receive honor. Similarly, the Holy Spirit derives great pleasure from seeing us cooperate with Him in glorifying Christ. He Himself wants to remain hidden, so that nothing diverts our gaze from the Lord Jesus.

Whenever we focus our attention on Christ, the Holy Spirit is in close partnership with us. The Spirit is pleased when we are glorifying the Lord. We can do this by:

- Observing the Lord's Supper to remember Christ in His suffering and death for our sins (1 Cor. 11:23-26).
- Making Jesus our example (Jn. 13:15; Phil. 2:5-11; 1 Pet. 2:21-24).
- Longing to know Christ better, so that we may be more like Him (Phil. 3:10-14).
- Not being afraid of dying because we're

looking forward to being with Christ
(2 Cor. 5:8; Phil. 1:21-23; 2 Tim. 4:6-8).

- Living in anticipation of the day we will appear at "the judgment seat of Christ" (2 Cor. 5:10).
- Being comforted by the fact that Christ is our intercessor in heaven (Heb. 4:14-16).
- Purifying ourselves from sin as we're living in the light of Christ's return (1 Jn. 3:2-3).
- Looking forward to Christ's rule over the earth (Isa. 2:1-4; Jer. 23:5-6; Rev. 20:1-4).
- Rejoicing in the assurance that every mortal being in God's universe will bow before Jesus Christ and confess Him as Lord (Phil. 2:9-11).

The Holy Spirit keeps Himself out of the limelight so that Christ may be honored. He is pleased when we praise and adore the Lord Jesus. He views us as partners with Him in glorifying Christ. Being Christ-centered, therefore, is an essential in being filled with the Spirit.

ESSENTIAL TWO:
Be In The Word

The Christian who wants to be Spirit-filled should be spending time in God's Word. His mind must be so filled with its truths that Bible passages automatically come to his mind when he encounters the situations of life. Just before Paul gave the command "do not be drunk with wine, in which is dissipation; but be filled with the Spirit," he wrote:

Therefore do not be unwise, but understand what the will of the Lord is (Eph. 5:17).

How do we know God's will? Primarily through the Scriptures, which came into existence when "holy men of God spoke as they were moved by the Holy Spirit" (2 Pet. 1:21).

The importance of the Bible in the Spirit-filled life was demonstrated by the Lord Jesus in His encounter with Satan at the beginning of His public ministry. Luke told us that Jesus was "filled with the Holy Spirit" when He entered into the wilderness for testing (Lk. 4:1-2). In response to each of Satan's temptations, our Lord answered by quoting the Scriptures—specifically Deuteronomy 8:3, 6:13, and 6:16. Since Jesus took on our genuine humanity, He "increased in wisdom and stature" (Lk. 2:52) like other boys. So we can be sure that He had to study to know the Scriptures. Christ's familiarity with the Bible, therefore, was an important element in His being "filled with the Holy Spirit."

As noted earlier, Paul pointed out the close relationship between "knowing what the will of the Lord is" and being "filled with the Holy Spirit" when he wrote Ephesians 5:17-18. He made the same connection in Colossians 3:16, which says:

Let the word of Christ dwell in you richly in all wisdom,
teaching and admonishing one another in psalms and
hymns and spiritual songs, singing with grace in your
hearts to the Lord.

The last part of this verse is almost identical to Ephesians 5:19-20 where Paul described the characteristics of a Spirit-filled Christian. In other words, letting the Word of Christ dwell in us richly is an essential in letting the Holy Spirit keep filling us.

If you want to be a Spirit-filled Christian, then, you must be in the Word of God. Give the Bible ample room in your life by reading it, studying it, and reflecting on it. The Scriptures were inspired by the Holy Spirit and are "profitable for doctrine, for reproof, for correction, for instruction in righteousness, that the man of God may be complete, thoroughly equipped for every good work" (2 Tim. 3:16-17).

Read the Bible! Study it! Be instructed by it! Obey its commands! Let it correct you! The Word of God has been given to make you a complete, well-equipped Christian. You cannot be Spirit-filled without it.

ESSENTIAL THREE:
Be Submissive

The third essential for a Spirit-filled life is to be submissive to God and His Word. Paul indicated this attitude of submission by the language he used when he wrote Ephesians 5:18. Translated literally, the latter part of this verse reads, "Keep letting the Holy Spirit fill you." We must continuously *allow* the Holy Spirit to fill us. We can do this only when we possess a submissive attitude toward Him.

The analogy Paul used of being drunk with wine carries the idea of submission. Paul wrote:

Do not get drunk with wine . . . but keep letting the Holy Spirit fill you [literal translation].

A person who is drunk is under the influence of alcohol. If he is very drunk, he is under its control. A person who keeps letting the Holy Spirit fill him will consciously, continuously, and voluntarily place himself under God's influence or control. No, he doesn't lose self-control. In fact, he exercises far more self-control than a person who does not possess the Holy Spirit. When a Christian consciously, continuously, and voluntarily submits to God, he is freed from slavery to the sinful habits and drives that once controlled him.

A person who keeps letting the Holy Spirit fill him will consciously, continuously, and voluntarily place himself under God's influence or control.

This attitude of submission is also present in Colossians 3:15–4:10, a passage that parallels Ephesians 5:18–6:9. When Paul told the believers in Colosse to place themselves under the rule of Christ's peace, and to give the Word of Christ a dominant place in their lives (3:16), he was calling for a submissive attitude. You place yourself under God's influence and control when you do these things. The result of letting the Holy Spirit keep filling you (Eph. 5:18) and letting the peace of Christ and the Word of Christ have dominance in your life (Col. 3:15-16) is the same—joy, mutual encouragement, praise, and gratitude.

When you have a submissive attitude toward God and His Word, the Holy Spirit can keep filling you. This is because:

- You place yourself under the authority of the Bible when it tells you to "put off" and "put to death" the sins of the flesh and to "put on" Christian virtues (Eph. 4:17–5:7; Col. 3:5-17).
- You humbly confess your sins so that you

will experience God's fellowship and cleansing
(1 Jn. 1:9).
- You submit to others as an expression of your
love for God, thus becoming a good marriage
partner, a good citizen, and a good representative of Christ (Eph. 5:2-33; 1 Pet. 2:11–3:17).

ESSENTIAL FOUR:
Be Confident

The fourth essential in being filled with the Spirit is to
be confident. When you have centered your life on
Jesus Christ, when you are in the Word and it is in you,
and when you have submitted to the Holy Spirit's leading, you can know that you have done your part. And,
having done that, you can be absolutely certain that
God has done His part. He has responded to you by filling you with His Spirit. Because of that:

- You don't need to wonder if you are spiritual
enough to be filled with the Spirit.
- You don't need to compare yourself with other
believers.
- You don't need to keep looking for some
spectacular sign from heaven.
- You don't need to wait for a great feeling of
tingling excitement to sweep over you.

Rather, you can know with absolute certainty that
because you are doing your part, God is doing His part.
And this confidence will help you live day-by-day in
the assurance that you are filled with the Holy Spirit.

But if you live with a defeatist attitude, it is probably
because you feel that you are losing your battle with sin.

Your lack of confidence, though, shows a failure to trust in the Lord's provision for you and in His power to _____ keep His part of the bargain.

You can know with absolute certainty that because you are doing your part, God is doing His part.

Look at the apostle Paul. Although he was very much aware of the power of the old nature and of the ongoing battle with the flesh, he was brimming with confidence. In Romans 7, for example, he was painfully honest in describing the battle between his old nature (the "law of sin") and his new nature (the "law of my mind"). But he then went right on to point out that the way of victory is through "Jesus Christ our Lord." He then said:

> *There is therefore now no condemnation to those who are in Christ Jesus. . . . For the law of the Spirit of life in Christ Jesus has made me free from the law of sin and death. For what the law could not do in that it was weak through the flesh, God did by sending His own Son in the likeness of sinful flesh, on account of sin: He condemned sin in the flesh, that the righteous requirement of the law might be fulfilled in us who do not walk according to the flesh but according to the Spirit (Rom. 8:1-4).*

This walking "in the Spirit" occurs when we are filled with the Spirit. It includes the four essentials we've just looked at in a blend of divine and human activity to overcome sin.

The walk in the Spirit is a walk of confidence in God. And this confidence produces spiritual victory because of:

- A continual awareness of the Spirit's presence (1 Cor. 6:19-20).
- A conscious dependence on the Spirit's power (Eph. 5:18).
- An acceptance of the Spirit's help in fulfilling the law of God (Rom. 8:4).
- A deliberate "putting off" of the flesh (Eph. 4:22).
- A willful rejection of sin (Rom. 6:1-2).
- A determined pursuit of what is right (Eph. 4:24).

The fourth essential in a Spirit-filled life, then, is confidence. This is especially true in our battle against sin. But when you have done your part—when you have repented of all known sin, confessed it, and replaced it with obedience to Christ—you can be certain that God has done His part in forgiving you and in giving you the power for spiritual victory. You can move ahead with your heart filled with confidence and the knowledge that you are filled with the Holy Spirit.

When you have repented of all known sin, confessed it, and replaced it with obedience to Christ, you can be certain that God has done His part in forgiving you and in giving you the power for spiritual victory.

HOW CAN I TELL WHEN I'M SPIRIT-FILLED?

Some people say that the way you can know you are filled with the Holy Spirit is to speak in tongues or to just "feel it." A woman called one of the counselors at RBC Ministries, for example, to say that she had times when she was so filled with the Holy Spirit that she couldn't speak a word of English. She said that anybody who doesn't speak in tongues is not Spirit-filled.

When Paul described the results of being filled with the Holy Spirit, however, he didn't mention tongues-speaking or a tingling feeling. But he did mention "speaking to one another in psalms and hymns and spiritual songs, singing and making melody in your heart to the Lord, giving thanks always for all things to God the Father in the name of our Lord Jesus Christ, submitting to one another in the fear of God" (Eph. 5:19-21; cp. Col. 3:16). He also listed nine fruit of the Spirit as evidence in Galatians 5:22-23.

FOUR EVIDENCES

According to Ephesians 5:19-21, a person who is filled with the Holy Spirit will know it because of four evidences in his life: joyful fellowship, heartfelt praise, abounding gratitude, and reverent submission. Let's look briefly at each of these.

1. **Joyful Fellowship.** The first evidence of being Spirit-filled is joyful fellowship with other Christians. Paul described it as "speaking to one another in psalms and hymns and spiritual songs" (v.19). The texts of these songs often take the form of mutual exhortation.

Singing with God's people had its roots in Hebrew worship. Psalms 29, 33, 37, 40, 95, 96, and 100 are only a few of the songs in which the Israelites encouraged one another to join together in praise, gratitude, and obedience.

Spirit-filled Christians love to sing with one another. For example, in our hymns we call on one another to praise the Lord: "Come we that love the Lord, and let our joys be known." We comfort one another: "God will take care of you." We challenge one another: "Must I go, and empty-handed?"

2. **Heartfelt Praise.** The second result of being filled with the Holy Spirit is heartfelt praise to God: "Singing and making melody in your heart to the Lord" (v.19). The term "in your heart" is sometimes taken as referring to singing on the inside, singing that isn't expressed outwardly. But that is unlikely. It probably means singing from a sincere heart, as expressed in Colossians 3:16, "Singing with grace in your hearts to the Lord."

3. **Abounding Gratitude.** The third evidence of being Spirit-filled is abounding gratitude: "Giving thanks always for all things to God the Father in the name of our Lord Jesus Christ" (v.20). In his letters, Paul repeatedly gave thanks to God, and he encouraged his readers to follow his example (Phil. 1:3; 4:6; Col. 1:3,12; 2:7; 3:15,17; 4:2; 1 Th. 1:2; 2:13; 5:18; 1 Tim. 1:12; 2:1; 4:3-4). He told us to give thanks to God in everything and for everything.

4. **Reverent Submission.** The fourth way we can know we are filled with the Holy Spirit is reverent submission: "Submitting to one another in the fear of God"

(v.21). A Spirit-filled person is humble, gentle, and meek. He is not proud, aggressive, or self-assertive. His reverence for Christ is the source of his humility. As a servant of Christ, he possesses a servant's spirit. Therefore, he does not find it difficult to submit to his fellow believers.

NINE FRUIT

In his letter to the Galatians, the apostle Paul pointed out that the life of a Spirit-filled person will be marked by nine moral qualities that he called "the fruit of the Spirit." When they are present, it is further evidence that a person is filled with the Holy Spirit. He wrote:

The fruit of the Spirit is love, joy, peace, longsuffering, kindness, goodness, faithfulness, gentleness, self-control. Against such there is no law (Gal. 5:22-23).

Let's look at each one of these spiritual qualities:

1. **Love:** an attitude that moves us to put God and others ahead of ourselves. A spirit that impels us to give, to serve, and to forgive.

2. **Joy:** a spirit of gladness rooted in our faith, expressed through song, and accompanied by an optimistic spirit.

3. **Peace:** inner serenity derived from God and based on the reality of our peace with God through Christ's sacrifice.

4. **Longsuffering:** patience in the midst of difficult circumstances and in our relationships with difficult people.

5. **Kindness:** practicing the golden rule of treating others as we expect them to treat us.

6. **Goodness:** open, honest, pure, and generous behavior.

7. **Faithfulness:** we can be trusted and depended on in all our relationships.

8. **Gentleness:** a tenderness of spirit that enables us to discipline others properly, to endure persecution graciously, and to witness to others sensitively.

9. **Self-control:** the quality that gives us control over our desires, especially those that relate to the body.

If the Holy Spirit is producing these nine moral qualities in your life, you are Spirit-filled. Paul's comment, "Against such there is no law" (v.23), means that nothing in the Mosaic law or any other law opposes these virtues or is needed to restrain them. In fact, when a person's life is marked by the four evidences of Ephesians 5:18-21 and the nine moral qualities of Galatians 5:22-23, the demands of the law are being fulfilled. When they are present, they provide evidence that you are filled with the Holy Spirit.

TWO WRONG ANSWERS

Anybody who reads widely or listens to many preachers will soon discover that conflicting answers are given to the question: "How can I be filled with the Holy Spirit?" Let's evaluate two wrong ideas that are being circulated today.

1. **"The Bible does not command us to be filled with the Holy Spirit."** Some Christian leaders do not emphasize the filling of the Holy Spirit. In fact, some even say that to talk about oneself as being Spirit-filled is a form

of spiritual pride. They acknowledge that in the book of Acts the apostles are sometimes described as "filled with the Spirit" or "full of the Holy Spirit." But they say that the Bible nowhere commands *us* to be filled with the Holy Spirit.

> *Some people say that to talk about oneself as being Spirit-filled is a form of spiritual pride.*

To support their claim, they point out that Ephesians 5:18 literally reads, "Do not be drunk with wine; but be filled *in spirit*." Because the word *spirit* is not modified by the word *Holy*, and because it has no article, they say Paul was talking about the human spirit.

Even if we grant the possibility that Ephesians 5:18 should be translated, "be filled in [your] spirit," we have ample biblical evidence for emphasizing the importance of a Spirit-filled life. In Galatians 5:16-26, Paul commanded us to "walk in the Spirit" and then told us that such a life will produce the "fruit of the Spirit."

In Romans 8:1-11, we are told that freedom from the power of indwelling sin comes to those who walk "according to the Spirit," the Spirit who is referred to as the indwelling "Spirit of God" and "Spirit of Christ" (v.9).

Furthermore, the terms *filled* and *full of* do refer to the Holy Spirit in other passages (Lk. 1:15,41,67; 4:1; Acts 2:4; 4:8,31; 6:3; 7:55; 9:17; 13:9), and the contrast between being drunk with wine and filled with the Holy Spirit was also given in Acts 2:13.

So, the teaching that every believer should be filled with the Holy Spirit does not stand or fall on one's interpretation of Ephesians 5:18. However, we are convinced that this verse does command every Christian to let the Holy Spirit keep filling him.

2. **"You need to seek a second blessing."** Followers of John Wesley, the Pentecostals, and the Charismatics believe that the filling of the Holy Spirit is a dramatic experience that takes place sometime after salvation. The Wesleyans prefer to speak of it as "entire sanctification," viewing it as a second work of grace in which the sin nature is removed and the Holy Spirit takes control. Pentecostals and Charismatics refer to it as a baptism of the Spirit, claiming that it is usually accompanied by speaking in tongues.

The problem with this view is that the New Testament never tells us to seek or anticipate a dramatic, post-salvation experience. We are justified the moment we believe (Rom. 5:1). And we receive the new birth and the permanent, indwelling Spirit at the instant of salvation (1 Cor. 6:19; 1 Pet. 1:22-23). True, we may have many wonderful experiences after salvation. And we may even have an encounter with the Lord that revolutionizes our way of life. But we have no biblical basis for expecting a second work of grace or a baptism of power that brings instant holiness. Rather, Paul called on us to "present [literally 'keep presenting'] your bodies a living sacrifice" (Rom. 12:1) and to "let the Holy Spirit keep filling you" (Eph. 5:18).

The New Testament never tells us to seek or anticipate a dramatic, post-salvation experience.

WHAT IS THE BAPTISM OF THE HOLY SPIRIT?

The baptism of the Holy Spirit is the act of the Holy Spirit by which He places a person into the church, the body of Christ. The first "baptism of the Holy Spirit took place in the upper room at Pentecost when the church began (Acts 2:1-13). Today it occurs the moment a person receives Jesus Christ as his Savior. Referring to this time when every believer is baptized by the Holy Spirit into the church, Paul wrote:

> *The baptism of the Holy Spirit is the act of the Holy Spirit by which He places a person into the church, the body of Christ.*

> *By one Spirit we were all baptized into one body (1 Cor. 12:13).*

Some Christians disagree. They maintain that the baptism of the Holy Spirit is the same as the filling of the Spirit. They say that it takes place sometime after salvation, and that it is accompanied by the sign of speaking in tongues. Those who hold this view say that their teaching is found in the book of Acts. But the phrase "baptized with the Holy Spirit" appears only twice in Acts (1:5; 11:16), and in neither place are we told that it is something we should seek sometime after salvation.

The baptism of the Holy Spirit was first announced by John the Baptist (Mt. 3:11; Mk. 1:8; Lk. 3:16; Jn. 1:33). And the Lord Jesus promised the baptism of the Holy Spirit before He ascended to heaven (Acts 1:4-5).

That promise was fulfilled on the Day of Pentecost, the day the church was born (Acts 2:1-13,32-33). The disciples were baptized into the church in the upper room. When Peter preached later that day, some 3,000 people believed (Acts 2:41-42). Then we are told:

> The Lord added to the church daily those who were being saved (2:47).

The book of Acts records three additional mini-Pentecosts. They took place with three different groups: the Samaritan believers, whose religion and ancestry were part Jewish (Acts 8:14-25); the Gentile family of Cornelius (10:44-48); and 12 people who had believed in Christ and received John's baptism but knew nothing about what had happened at Pentecost (19:1-7). When Peter saw that the Holy Spirit had come upon the Gentiles, he remembered the Spirit-baptism promised by Christ. He wrote:

A Christian who is looking for the baptism of the Holy Spirit is wasting his time looking for something he already has.

> Then I remembered the word of the Lord, how He said, "John indeed baptized with water, but you shall be baptized with the Holy Spirit." If therefore God gave them the same gift as He gave us when we believed on the Lord Jesus Christ, who was I that I could withstand God? (Acts 11:16-17).

By giving visible signs in these three instances the Holy Spirit confirmed the fact that Jesus Christ was building His church. These signs were given during the transition from the Jewish beginnings of the church to the full inclusion of the Gentiles. When the transition was over, the baptism of the Holy Spirit was no longer accompanied by visible signs. When a person trusts Christ today, he is placed into the church, the body of Christ, that very moment. Paul wrote:

> For by one Spirit we were all baptized into one body— whether Jews or Greeks, whether slaves or free—and have all been made to drink into one Spirit (1 Cor. 12:13).

The words translated "we were all baptized" speak of an action that took place in one instant of time. The baptism of the Spirit takes place at the moment of salvation, is not repeated, and is not to be sought after salvation. The baptism of the Holy Spirit, therefore, is the placing of the believer into the body of Christ by the Holy Spirit at the moment of salvation.

The baptism of the Spirit takes place at the moment of salvation, is not repeated, and is not to be sought after salvation.

Checklist For Being Spirit-Filled

As you think through the whole topic of being filled with the Holy Spirit, you may wonder where you are spiritually. Answering the following questions honestly will help you evaluate your relationship to the Holy Spirit:

- ❏ I have submitted to the Holy Spirit, asking Him to lead me.
- ❏ I am learning from the Bible through regular reading, study, and meditation.
- ❏ I am relying on the Holy Spirit to help me overcome my sinful desires.
- ❏ I enjoy getting together with God's people for fellowship, Bible study, and prayer.
- ❏ People who know me think of me as a happy, joyous Christian.
- ❏ When trouble comes, I am at peace in my innermost being.
- ❏ When I become aware of sin in my life, I immediately confess it and ask God to help me to gain the victory.
- ❏ I am gentle in my relationships with other people and patient with God.
- ❏ I can point to certain times when the Holy Spirit has given me the power to perform a certain task or carry a heavy burden.
- ❏ I am growing in self-control.

"A Spirit-Filled Man"

A good friend of our RBC Ministries staff says he feels uncomfortable about saying that he is a man who is filled with the Holy Spirit. He says that it would bother him if someone were to introduce him from the pulpit as "a Spirit-filled man of God" before he began speaking. He adds that he struggled with the concept of being filled with the Spirit as a young man. He wrote:

> For more than 45 years I have wrestled with this matter of being Spirit-filled. As a young man of 18, I often passed out tracts on street corners and preached in open air meetings. I knew I needed the Holy Spirit and I asked Him to help me. But I felt so unworthy, and I wondered how He could ever use a person like me. Yet, in spite of my feelings about myself, He blessed my efforts and people were saved.
>
> When I was 23 years old and in the army, I went forward in a Pentecostal church to receive what they called the "baptism of the Holy Spirit." But things didn't change very much. And when I attended a Bible school later, I learned that I already had the baptism of the Spirit when I trusted in Christ years before. As I reflected, I realized that I was probably looking for the assurance that the Holy Spirit was really operating in my life.

"As I reflected, I realized that I was probably looking for the assurance that the Holy Spirit was really operating in my life."

This man's experience is probably similar to that of

many young Christians who want to please and obey the Lord. But he has been serving the Lord for many years. How does he feel today? He said:

Through the years, the Lord has given me the joy of an assured and victorious Christian life. He has given me a satisfying and fruitful ministry. He has used me to help people trust in Christ as their personal Savior and then to help them grow in their faith. I have seen spiritual victories won and Satan defeated. In that sense, I can say that I know the blessing of being filled with the Holy Spirit.

But I'm still far from being perfect in my private life and in my work. Because of that, I would still be embarrassed to be called a Spirit-filled man. I know that I am sometimes selfish or envious. I think worldly thoughts. I'm inclined to be too competitive. Sometimes I feel terribly sinful.

We who know this man consider him to be Spirit-filled. We all feel that he is a man of God. He grieves over sin. He submits to the Spirit's leading. He studies the Bible diligently and does his best to obey it. And he is generous and compassionate. We all agree that he is a man who is filled with the Holy Spirit.

Being filled with the Spirit is not something you'd normally say about yourself.

But he's probably right—being filled with the Spirit is not something you'd normally say about yourself. It's like saying, "I'm humble." You just don't talk about yourself that way. But we can say of him with confidence, "He's a Spirit-filled man."

A FINAL WORD

We have seen that to be filled with the Holy Spirit we must be Christ-centered, in the Word, submissive, and confident.

What about you? If you are a Christian, being filled with the Spirit is not an option, it's a command. Is Christ at the center of your thoughts and aspirations? Are you trying to follow His example? Are you spending time studying the Bible so that your mind is saturated with God's truth and His will for your life? Are you yielded and submissive to God? Are you confessing your sins? Are you sensitive to the Spirit's leading so that you are not quenching His power in you? Do you have the confident assurance that you are Spirit-filled when you are Christ-centered, in the Word, and submissive? If you can answer yes, you are Spirit-filled and His fruit will be evident in your life.

But perhaps you are not a Christian. If you have never trusted Christ as your Savior, you cannot be filled with the Holy Spirit because He is not in you. To bring Him into your life, you need to admit your sin and inability to save yourself (Eph. 2:8-9) and ask Christ to save you. He has promised to save all who desire to turn from their sins and call in faith on Him. The Bible says:

As many as received Him, to them He gave the right to become children of God, even to those who believe in His name (Jn. 1:12).

Trust Christ today. Then you'll have taken the first step to being filled with the Holy Spirit.

THREE

SHOULD WE EXPECT MORE FROM THE SPIRIT?

Signs and wonders accompanied Christ's first disciples. Should we expect the same evidence of the Spirit's power today? A growing number of people are saying yes.

In the following pages, Kurt De Haan responds to those who are caught in the difficult tension of wanting to believe that "all things are possible" without being presumptuous before God or gullible before man.

It is our prayer that this chapter will help us to be ready for anything God wants to do, while alerting us to the danger of those who claim miracles that are hard to see or prove. May we not be a generation that has a sign and doesn't believe it or one that wants a sign and doesn't need it.

Martin R. De Haan II

WHAT'S THE ANSWER?

Something was wrong but I couldn't figure out what it was. The family station wagon would hardly start—if at all. I had bought a new battery just a few months earlier, and a rebuilt alternator the previous year. I drove to see an auto mechanic. After checking out the car, he concluded that the problem was a slightly loose belt. He tightened it, charged the battery, and gave me a bill.

A few weeks later, though, the car again had problems starting. It just didn't have starting power. Because of a recently blown fuse, I figured that the problem was a short circuit. So I pulled fuses and checked wiring, but no obvious problem surfaced.

Back to the auto mechanic I went. This time he did a few more tests. My guess had been wrong. And so was his first diagnosis. This time he discovered the real culprit—a defective battery. Even though it was fairly new, it wouldn't hold enough power to keep my car operating properly. It had to be replaced. And what a difference a good battery made! The power was back!

Some days we just can't seem to get started doing what we know we should do for the Lord. We may know that the Bible says the Holy Spirit indwells Christ's followers, but we may not sense the difference His presence makes. When we read the New Testament, we may conclude that we lack the kind of spiritual power that surged through the early church.

It may be that we, family, or friends are struggling with emotional, physical, or spiritual problems that just don't seem to be getting any better. We see believers who seem to be losing the fight against the forces of evil. Our society is deteriorating. Maybe we are frustrated because our witness and service lack power. Our times of worship may be routines mired in tired traditions. Our faith may seem ineffective in relating to the real world of child-training, strained marriage relationships, temptations, addictions, injustices, debilitating illnesses, and the pressures of the workplace.

Is there more to the Christian life than what you and I are experiencing? Probably. Even the spiritually mature apostle Paul longed for a deeper and greater relationship with Jesus (Phil. 3:10). And he prayed that fellow believers would know Christ better and experience more fully the power of God's Spirit in their lives (Eph. 1:17-19).

Many individuals and groups today are telling us how to live more powerful Christian lives. But not all of them have a solid biblical basis. We need to be discerning, careful that we don't accept "quick fixes" that don't get

Many believers long for an elusive "something more" in their Christian lives.

at the root of the problem. We certainly don't need a diagnosis that harms instead of helps.

To avoid the extremes of either becoming content with an anemic, passive Christianity, or seeking a type of power and spiritual experience God never promised to give us, we need to know what the Bible says we can expect from the Holy Spirit.

WHAT MORE DO WE NEED?

I've heard or read similar stories over and over again: Followers of Jesus tell how they came to a point in their life when they longed for a more intimate relationship with the Lord, for more meaningful worship, or for greater effectiveness in their service or evangelism. Then they found "something more." What they found has many different forms.

Some find what they are looking for in what we might consider a cult. There they may discover strong leadership, a sense of community, a unique identity, and fresh "revelations" to supplement (or even overrule) the Bible.

Even within orthodox Christianity, the search for more has led people in different directions. One new denomination promotes traditional forms of worship they claim have been handed down from the early church. They find greater security in a very structured organization, predictable worship, and strong authority.

Still other believers desire to break free of tradition and allow greater spontaneity and individual expression. Among these people are those who seek dramatic experiences in which they mystically sense the Holy Spirit's power at work.

This is a crucial topic that we need to understand. After all, how we relate to the Holy Spirit is the heart of the Christian life. The New Testament emphasizes the importance of the Spirit's work in our lives. For example:

- "It is the Spirit who gives life" (Jn. 6:63).
- "[The Father] will give you another Helper, that He may abide with you forever—the

Spirit of truth; . . . He dwells with you and will be in you" (Jn. 14:16-17).

- "You shall receive power when the Holy Spirit has come upon you; and you shall be witnesses to Me" (Acts 1:8).
- "They were all filled with the Holy Spirit, and they spoke the Word of God with boldness" (Acts 4:31).
- "If anyone does not have the Spirit of Christ, he is not His" (Rom. 8:9).

Our relationship to the Spirit is the heart of the Christian life.

- "If you live according to the flesh you will die; but if by the Spirit you put to death the deeds of the body, you will live. For as many as are led by the Spirit of God, these are sons of God" (Rom. 8:13-14).
- "The Spirit also helps in our weaknesses. For we do not know what we should pray for as we ought, but the Spirit Himself makes intercession for us" (Rom. 8:26).
- "We have received, not the spirit of the world, but the Spirit who is from God, that we might know the things that have been freely given to us by God" (1 Cor. 2:12).
- "Your body is the temple of the Holy Spirit who is in you" (1 Cor. 6:19).
- "The manifestation of the Spirit is given to each one for the profit of all" (1 Cor. 12:7).
- "Having begun in the Spirit, are you now being made perfect by the flesh?" (Gal. 3:3).

- "Walk in the Spirit, and you shall not fulfill the lust of the flesh" (Gal. 5:16).
- "The fruit of the Spirit is love, joy, peace, longsuffering, kindness, goodness, faithfulness, gentleness, self-control" (Gal. 5:22-23).
- "Since we live by the Spirit, let us keep in step with the Spirit" (Gal. 5:25 NIV).
- "Be filled with the Spirit" (Eph. 5:18).
- "[Pray] in the Spirit" (Eph. 6:18).
- "We know that He abides in us, by the Spirit whom He has given us" (1 Jn. 3:24).
- "He who is in you is greater than he who is in the world" (1 Jn. 4:4).

As you can see, the Holy Spirit has a vital role in our lives. We need a greater appreciation of His power in us. We would be foolish not to be open and submissive to His work in us individually and as churches.

But how does the Spirit work? Do we sometimes expect too little from Him, or more than God has clearly promised He would do? By going to either extreme we may find ourselves actually hindering the Spirit we think we are honoring.

As we examine this topic of what we should expect from the Holy Spirit, we will look at four issues that have been the focus of discussion and even controversy. We will seek to answer these four questions:

1. Do we need more signs?
2. Do we need more revelations?
3. Do we need more healings?
4. Do we need more weapons?

MORE SIGNS?

Can you imagine the look on the faces of the 5,000-plus people who saw Jesus multiply five loaves and two fish? (Jn. 6). What an incredible sight that must have been! It was an awesome display of the Holy Spirit's power working through Jesus, backing His claim to be the promised Messiah.

Jesus' 3-year ministry was punctuated by many miracles. He demonstrated power over nature by:

- calming a storm (Mt. 8:23-27)
- walking on water (Mt. 14:25)
- multiplying food (Mt. 14:15-21; 15:32-38)
- pulling a coin from a fish's mouth (Mt. 17:24-27)
- causing a fig tree to wither (Mt. 21:18-22)
- catching fish (Lk. 5:4-11; Jn. 21:1-11)
- turning water into wine (Jn. 2:1-11)

Jesus healed people of:

- leprosy (Mt. 8:2-4; Lk. 17:11-19)
- paralysis (Mt. 8:5-13; 9:1-8; Jn. 5:1-9)
- fever (Mt. 8:14-17; Jn. 4:46-51)
- demon possession (Mt. 8:28-34; 9:32-33; 15:21-28; 17:14-18; Mk. 1:23-26)
- chronic bleeding (Mt. 9:20-22)
- blindness (Mt. 9:27-31; 12:22; 20:29-34; Mk. 8:22-26)
- a shriveled hand (Mt. 12:10-13)
- deafness (Mk. 7:31-37)
- crippled limbs (Lk. 13:11-13)
- dropsy (Lk. 14:1-4)
- a severed ear (Lk. 22:50-51)

Jesus also brought dead people back to life (Mt. 9:18-

25; Lk. 7:11-15; Jn. 11:1-44). And He Himself rose from the grave in the power of the Spirit (Mt. 28; Rom. 1:4; Eph. 1:19-20).

Why did Jesus do so many miracles?

Miracles occurred throughout biblical history but mostly in clusters during times when God was revealing significant new information and authenticating the messengers. Those major periods were: (1) the Exodus and the establishment of Israel as a nation under the leadership of Moses and Joshua, (2) the time of the prophets Elijah and Elisha, and (3) the coming of Jesus and the establishment of the church through the apostles.

The signs and wonders Jesus performed gave ample evidence that He was who He claimed to be. As the One who did signs and wonders, the One who fulfilled Old Testament prophecies, the One who lived a perfect life, the One who rose from the grave, and the One who will return to set up His kingdom on earth, Jesus is supremely worthy of our complete trust.

John ended his Gospel with the reason why he documented Jesus' miracles. He wrote:

Jesus did many other signs . . . ; but these are written that you may believe that Jesus is the Christ, the Son of God, and that believing you may have life in His name (Jn. 20:30-31).

How did the apostles duplicate Jesus' ministry?

On various occasions Jesus empowered others to carry out His ministry. He sent out His 12 disciples on a special mission to the Jews and gave them the power to cast out demons and heal diseases (Lk. 9:1-6). Later, Jesus appointed 70 others, sending them out two by two to the cities where He was about to go (Lk. 10). They were to proclaim that the kingdom of God was near (v.9), they were to heal the sick (v.9), and they were given authority to defeat demons (vv.17-19).

The book of Acts records several instances in which the apostles were involved in healing and casting out demons (3:2-16; 5:12-16; 9:36-42; 20:6-12; 28:1-6). These miracles served to give credence to the apostles' message. Only two non-apostles were said to have performed miracles: the specially commissioned "deacons," Stephen and Philip (Acts 6:5,8; 8:5-13).

The apostles had a unique function in the establishing of the early church. Ephesians 2:20 states that the church was "built on the foundation of the apostles and prophets, Jesus Christ Himself being the chief cornerstone." The apostle Paul spoke of miracles as being the mark of a true apostle. As he described his own ministry, he wrote, "Truly the signs of an apostle were accomplished among you with all perseverance, in signs and wonders and mighty deeds" (2 Cor. 12:12).

Some religious groups are claiming that all believers today have the same mission the apostles did. But nowhere in the New Testament do we find believers in general performing the types of dramatic miracles of the apostles. The apostles were uniquely commissioned for the founding stage of the church.

> *Nowhere in the New Testament do we find believers in general performing the types of dramatic miracles of the apostles.*

How did the early church experience the miraculous power of God's Spirit?

In addition to the work of the 12 disciples of Christ and the 70 special ambassadors, Christ gifted certain people in the early church to carry on special ministries. These gifts of the Spirit are included among the list of the gifts in 1 Corinthians 12. The ones that cause the most debate today are "gifts of healings," "working of miracles," "prophecy," "tongues," and "interpretation of tongues" (vv.9-10).

Some Christians say that these gifts are no longer active in the church today, that they died out in the first century because their purpose had been served. Others believe that these gifts fell into disuse because the church quickly became secularized and in need of revival. Those who say that such gifts are valid today point to periods of recent history in which believers felt they had experienced a special working of the Spirit— whether healings, prophecies, or tongues-speaking.

In the middle of the second century, some believers, longing for the experiences of the apostolic church, reacted against a growing formalism that seemed to stifle church life. A man named Montanus, who lived in central Asia Minor, thought he had the answer to the church's problems.

According to historian Howard Vos, the Montanist movement emphasized special spiritual gifts, and in some areas required strict self-denial in an effort to please God. Vos states:

> Though generally orthodox, its emphasis on
> such spiritual gifts as continuance of prophetic

revelation and its requirement of ascetic practices as if they were truths of revelation caused it to be condemned. The church declared that biblical revelation had come to an end and that special spiritual gifts were no longer operative (*Beginnings In Church History*, Moody Press, 1977, p.39).

Some movements in the church today have much in common with Montanism. They emphasize the continuance or revival of all the gifts of the Spirit. They focus on demonstrations of God's power—especially in physical healings and the deliverance of people from demonic influence. They tell us that to evangelize effectively we need dramatic displays. They encourage ecstatic experiences as evidences of the Spirit's presence. They want to be more open to direct revelations and Spirit-given impressions.

What gifts do we need today?

This is a tough question to answer because I'm sure that neither you nor I would ever want to be guilty of putting any limitations on what we think God can or wants to do. Another problem is that it's difficult to verify the claims of those who say they possess some of the more spectacular gifts.

> *"The manifestation of the Spirit is given to each one for the profit of all."*
> (1 COR. 12:7)

We also have to keep in mind that the Bible does not appear to give us a strict cataloging of all the abilities that He will bestow on believers for the good of the church. The lists of spiritual gifts are given in only three places in the New Testament (see Rom. 12:6-8; 1 Cor. 12:8-10,28-30; Eph. 4:11), and the items mentioned vary a great deal. There is no indication that we should adopt any one of these lists as a once-for-all catalog of how the Spirit will work in every generation.

Among the gifts are those that had a definite purpose in the founding and establishing of the early church: apostles and prophets (Eph. 2:20). Tongues-speaking and prophecy also had a role in assisting the early believers before they had an established collection of New Testament writings.

Other gifts, such as teaching, helping, serving, showing mercy, exhorting, administrating, exercising wisdom or spiritual knowledge, giving, evangelizing, and pastoring seem to have a timeless application throughout church history. And these are commonly expressed in churches today.

Some gifts, such as miracles and healings, also seemed to play a crucial role in the founding of the church, and have found only sporadic expression in the history of the church. (We will examine the topic of healing on pages 97-102.)

What signs of the Holy Spirit's activity should we expect to see?

Before Jesus left this earth, He announced that after He was gone He would send the Spirit (Jn. 14:16-17; 16:7; Acts 1:4-8). During this period between the first and second comings of Christ, the Holy Spirit is actively working to bring conviction of sin, to give spiritual life, and to assist believers in living in a way that gives glory to Jesus. The Spirit's primary mission is to carry out Christ's orders (Jn. 16:12-15).

We don't need dramatic "signs and wonders" to mature or minister. Church services should not be a setting for out-of-control experiences under the guise of "allowing the Spirit to do His work." Our Lord is a God of order (1 Cor. 14:40), and He produces the fruit of self-control (Gal. 5:23).

When people asked Jesus for a sign, He told them that "an evil and adulterous generation seeks after a sign" (Mt. 12:39). They were curious but not ready to repent and follow Him. The same problem exists today among believers who want a show of supernatural power but who have little desire to involve themselves in the spiritual self-discipline necessary for personal growth.

> "An evil and adulterous generation seeks after a sign."
> JESUS (MT. 12:39)

As the gospel truth is introduced into cultures dominated by demonic activity, God may display His power dramatically. Missionaries sometimes recount dramatic "power encounters" as the gospel is introduced into pagan cultures. But this is the exception, not a normal everyday experience. We would be wrong to deny the possibility that God could perform a dramatic miracle to give credence to a missionary, but we would be just as wrong to expect such situations to occur regularly.

In the days preceding Christ's return, we can expect signs from false prophets and teachers who want people to think of them as "ministers of righteousness" (2 Cor. 11:13-15). Jesus warned, "False christs and false prophets will rise and show great signs and wonders to deceive, if possible, even the elect" (Mt. 24:24).

What if I don't have a dramatic spiritual experience?

Despite all the protests to the contrary, those who promote the experiences of tongues, healings, prophetic utterances, words of knowledge, and ecstatic feelings do exert an intimidating force on those who do not share their experiences or who question their validity. I personally have felt intimidated as I have read books and listened to speakers who promote unusual experiences.

The apostle Paul warned the Corinthian believers against false teachers who were trying to force them into submission with incredible claims of spiritual authority (2 Cor. 11:1-15). They claimed to be superior even to Paul! The apostle sarcastically called them

> *"I am afraid that . . . your minds may somehow be led astray from your sincere and pure devotion to Christ."*
> PAUL (2 COR. 11:3 NIV)

"super-apostles" (v.5 NIV). He was concerned that the believers might be led astray from the simple truth of the gospel.

We would be naive to think that we do not face the same threat today. That is why we must carefully examine our faith, evaluate what we are being told, and test all things by what God has said in His sure and trustworthy Word. We would be wise to evaluate all teaching by the sure Word of God, as the Bereans did. They "searched the Scriptures" to see if what the apostle Paul preached to them was true (Acts 17:11).

MORE REVELATIONS?

Have you ever tried to bake a cake without a recipe? Program a video cassette recorder (VCR) without an instruction booklet? Sew a dress without a pattern? Train children without some advice? Find an address in an unfamiliar city without a map? Live the Christian life without being taught how?

In order to know God and to live in a way that pleases Him, we need information. Directions for knowing God don't come built-in when we are born. In fact, we wouldn't know enough about the Lord to appreciate His greatness, our need of salvation, and how to find acceptance with Him if it were not for His self-disclosure down through history through special appearances, angelic messengers, prophets, apostles, and the collection of inspired writings we call the Bible.

Is God continuing to author more Scripture? Is He speaking through modern-day Elijahs or Jeremiahs? Is He giving special impressions to some people for their own good or the good of their church? How much new information is He disclosing? When people stand up during our meetings and give the rest of the congregation a direct "word from the Lord" concerning a vote on an annual budget or building project or calling a new pastor, should we believe them?

The answers to the above questions are not as neat

and tidy as we might like them to be. But I believe the Bible gives us some guidelines by which to judge the validity of modern-day claims.

Does the Bible tell us enough about God?

According to the apostle Paul, the written Word contains everything we need for knowing God and living in a way that pleases Him. Paul wrote:

All Scripture is given by inspiration of God, and is profitable for doctrine, for reproof, for correction, for instruction in righteousness, that the man of God may be complete, thoroughly equipped for every good work (2 Tim. 3:16-17).

The Bible gives us doctrinal truth, points out heresy, corrects wrong behavior, and tells us how to live in a way that pleases the Lord. Such truths, Paul said, are sufficient to bring us to spiritual maturity and thoroughly equip us for life. Our real problem today is not a lack of information but a lack of reading and obeying the clear instruction He has already given to us.

Yet from time to time throughout history, certain individuals and groups have claimed that they received additional information directly from God. One of the earliest examples of this was the sect founded by Montanus, whom we referred to earlier (pp.86-87). As early as the second century, people felt a need for new revelation. And because the collection of New Testament Scriptures had not yet been formally ratified and recognized, many people were unsure whether God was continuing to speak through prophets.

According to Harold O. J. Brown, Montanus "considered himself the last great prophet, who would be immediately followed by the establishment of the heavenly Jerusalem." He thought he had a special prophetic gift, which he shared with two prophetesses, Maximilla and Prisca. Brown explains, "The Montanists . . . were orthodox with respect to their doctrine of God . . . and merely wanted to intensify it by adding their new revelation" (*Heresies*, Doubleday, 1984, pp.66-67).

Within the Christian church today, among those who profess strong faith in the orthodox truths about God, there are believers who think (as did Montanus) that they are experiencing an outpouring of the Spirit in the last days. But Montanism was declared heretical, and the sufficiency of Scripture was emphasized. Should we do less today?

The many cultic groups that have grown up since the first century have also claimed additional special revelation from God. Though they use the Bible and talk about Christ, they add their own authoritative teachings, which often contradict the Bible.

How can we test someone who claims to be a prophet?

In Deuteronomy 18, the Lord gave tests of a true prophet:

The prophet who presumes to speak a word in My name, which I have not commanded him to speak, or who speaks in the name of other gods, that prophet shall die. And if you say in your heart, "How shall we know the word which the Lord has not spoken?"—when a prophet speaks in the name of the Lord, if the thing does not happen or come to pass, that is the thing which the Lord has not spoken; the prophet has spoken it presumptuously; you shall not be afraid of him (Dt. 18:20-22).

Do modern-day prophets pass this test? Do their prophecies come true? Or are they as reliable as astrologers? By their own admission, many modern-day prophets avoid the 100-percent-accuracy test by redefining prophecy for today. They say that the gift of prophecy is less authoritative, so the Old Testament test does not apply. And when a "prophet" speaks inaccurately, his defenders say that God's messages sometimes get garbled by the messenger. But this redefining seems to be an attempt to justify the current craving for more words from God even though modern prophets have a poor track record.

> **Prophet**—one who spoke by direct inspiration on God's behalf, communicating the Spirit-led message (2 Pet. 1:21).
>
> **Prophecy**—the message/words of a prophet. Depending on the situation, this message took the form of a prediction, direction, correction, or encouragement.
>
> **Gift Of Prophecy**—In the New Testament church, this was evident in foretelling the future and a special ability to edify believers by conveying authoritative messages from the Lord.

Neil Babcox was the pastor of a church in Illinois that believed that God was speaking through believers in modern-day prophecy. In fact, he sought the gift and believed that God was speaking through him and others at various times for the building up of the local group of believers. But then, Babcox writes:

What had started as a romantic venture, an idealistic quest for spiritual gifts, was slowly, imperceptibly changing. Into what I wasn't sure. All I knew was that the excitement and romance of prophesying was turning into an uneasy sense that the prophecies I heard, including my own, were hardly worthy of the name. The idea that they were the words of the living God was beginning to seem painfully ludicrous. . . .

In my case, there were four simple words that played a decisive role in changing my heart: *thus saith the Lord*. To me, these were the most unsettling words. . . . I could not help but think that if the prophecies spoken in our church were actually related to the prophecies recorded in Scripture, then they were distant relatives indeed. . . . What evidence was there that we were not just following our own spirits instead of the Spirit of God? I could find no evidence in the Bible that prophecies were communicated by mere intuition or subjective impressions. And yet, in nearly all cases this is how ours were received. And these impressions and intuitions could not be authenticated in any kind of objective sense (*A Search For Charismatic Reality*, Multnomah Press, 1985, pp.52,53-55).

In sharp contrast, the Old Testament prophet Ezekiel had no question that the Lord was speaking through him, and he condemned the phony prophets. He said:

The word of the Lord came to me, saying, "Son of man, prophesy against the prophets of Israel who prophesy, and say to those who prophesy out of their own heart, 'Hear the word of the Lord!'" Thus says the Lord God: "Woe to the foolish prophets, who follow their own spirit and have seen nothing!" (Ezek. 13:1-3).

Should we expect direct messages from God via audible voices or impressions?

Has God promised to speak to us in this manner? Several books have been written recently about hearing the voice of God through subjective impressions. Much of what they say is commendable when it comes to nurturing a close relationship with Christ and depending on the indwelling Spirit. What the authors have to say about the need for meditation on Scripture and heartfelt prayer is often excellent. But then they take a leap away from what the Bible says we can expect by saying that we all can experience intimate conversations with God. According to the examples some authors give, God gives instructions on such matters as how to fix leaky plumbing and how to deal with specific child-training issues.

Undoubtedly, God can speak to us through impressions. He can guide our thoughts so that we know what to say in witnessing situations. He can help us to find solutions to knotty problems. He can guide our ministry efforts. But nowhere in the Bible are we promised the kind of impressions that give us the right to tell others, "The Lord said" you should do this or that. Let's be careful that we do not put words in His mouth. Do we realize what an awesome claim it is to profess to speak for God?

Let's not be intimidated into accepting every self-proclaimed prophet just because we don't want to be guilty of silencing the Lord. When the Lord speaks, we will have no doubt about it. True prophecy welcomes examination and will stand the test (1 Th. 5:21; 1 Jn. 4:1).

MORE HEALINGS?

I was flipping across the channels on my TV set when I noticed a heavily perspiring preacher roaming a stage in a large auditorium. I sat back and listened to what was going on.

After pausing to wipe his brow and pat his neck with a large white handkerchief, the speaker mentioned to the audience that he felt God wanted him to ask any people who had cancer to come to the front of the auditorium because God wanted to heal them. Then he turned to the camera and said that anyone in the auditorium or watching TV who believed that God would want a person to suffer from cancer was horribly wrong. His God, he said, would never purposely send suffering into a person's life. He even said he would never serve a God who would do such a thing. His God, he bellowed, was the God who heals our sicknesses and who will heal our cancers if we just believe and ask Him to. The telecast ended as he laid his hands on each person and prayed for healing. He implied that they would be healed—no doubt about it.

What do you think? Was he acting in faith or parading in presumption? Let's examine some passages of Scripture and answer some crucial questions as we try to arrive at a perspective that above all recognizes God's power and plan for our health in this world.

Why do we get sick? Why do we die?

Should we expect God to spare us from sickness and death because Jesus died on the cross for our sins? I find it interesting that some preachers who say God wants us to enjoy good health are able to separate sickness from death. I've never heard a person say that you won't die if you simply ask God to keep you alive. Yet the same logic is applied to sickness.

> *I've never heard a person say that you won't die if you simply ask God to keep you alive.*

It is said that we need not be sick if we simply ask God for healing.

To deal with this issue, we need to step back and review why people get sick and die. In the beginnings of human history, Adam and Eve didn't have to worry about the flu or about buying life insurance. They would have lived forever in perfect health if they had not disobeyed God's command not to eat the fruit of the one forbidden tree. But when they took of the forbidden fruit, they were destined to die. The effects of their willful act of sin reverberated through every atom of the universe. Thereafter, weeds, pain, and death would be an inescapable part of human existence.

Throughout the Old Testament we find sickness and death. On occasion God miraculously healed (Num.

12:10-15; 21:6-9; 1 Ki. 13:3-6; Is. 38:21), and a few times He even raised a person from the dead (1 Ki. 17:17-23; 2 Ki. 4:32-37; 13:21).

Why were there so many healings during the time of Jesus and the apostles?

When we come to the New Testament Gospels, we are struck by the abundance of healings that Jesus and His disciples performed. It seems that wherever Jesus went He preached the good news of the kingdom and healed people.

Signs and wonders accompanied the ministry of Jesus and were the marks of an apostle (2 Cor. 12:12). They were never promised to believers at large. As the later books of the New Testament were written, we do not read much about the spectacular and miraculous. The outpouring of miracles that accompanied Jesus' ministry and the initial extension of the gospel into new lands seemed to taper off. The later books of the New Testament seem rather uneventful compared to the drama and exciting accounts of the miraculous in the early years of the church as the apostles ministered. Never again in the history of the church has any period rivaled the incredible miracles during the time of Christ and the apostles.

> *Signs and wonders accompanied the ministry of Jesus and were the marks of an apostle. They were never promised to believers at large.*

The contrast between the so-called healing ministries of today and the healing ministry of Jesus and the apostles is sharp. Most healings today seem to be of the psychosomatic, hard-to-prove variety. That does not mean that God does not heal today—He certainly can and does—but we need to be cautious about the claims of healers.

We have no reason to expect that in this life we will escape all sickness or that we will not die. We are living with unglorified bodies in a world that has been devastated by the effects of sin and the work of Satan. Any physical healing that God chooses to give is merely a temporary solution, because everyone eventually dies of something.

Can't we do something about sickness and suffering?

Yes we can—and we should. We should pray for the sick and strive for health in all areas of personal life and in our society. We should not hesitate to ask the Lord to grant us relief from suffering. Unfortunately, we are often too reluctant to believe that God has the power to heal. We pray for the skill of the doctors, for the effectiveness of the medicine, and for comfort for the sick person, but we tend to neglect to ask God for more direct restoration to health.

James, near the close of his short letter, has some crucial words for us to consider. He wrote:

Is anyone among you suffering? Let him pray. Is anyone cheerful? Let him sing psalms. Is anyone among you sick? Let him call for the elders of the church, and let them pray over him, anointing him with oil in the name of the Lord.

And the prayer of faith will save the sick, and the Lord will raise him up. And if he has committed sins, he will be forgiven (Jas. 5:13-15).

The meaning and application of these verses have been debated by Bible scholars, but we can be confident of the following principles:

1. If you are suffering or sick, you should pray
2. Ask trusted, mature believers to pray for you.
3. Believe that God has the power to heal you if that is what He chooses to do.
4. As you pray and talk to others about your illness, it is appropriate to evaluate your relationship to the Lord to see if your illness is due to the effects of deliberate sin and God's chastening. If so, you must confess your sin.

What do we know for sure?

The RBC publication *Does God Want Me Well?* (Q0104) offers four answers (pp.7-17):

1. "God will make you well." Either in this life or the next, God will relieve your suffering (1 Cor. 15; 2 Cor. 4:16–5:1).
2. "God hurts when you hurt." This truth is demonstrated powerfully in the life and death of God's Son, Jesus Christ. Jesus endured physical pain and suffering. He knows very well what you and I are going through (Heb. 4:15-16).
3. "God knows why you're suffering." Even though Job didn't understand why he had to endure incredible hardships and physical pain, God knew. Sometimes we have disobeyed basic rules of good health. Or

we could be sick because we are living in sin, and God is disciplining us (1 Cor. 11:29-30; Heb. 12:6). God does not promise anyone a suffering-free life. And if He allows pain in our lives, we can be sure He has good reasons.

4. "God is in control." This doesn't mean that God is the direct cause of every injury or disease. Sometimes Satan is to blame, as are natural laws that God has built into the universe.

No matter what God chooses to do—whether He chooses to heal or not—we can be sure He will give us the grace to handle whatever He decides. The apostle Paul, after praying repeatedly that the Lord would remove an ailment from him, said that the Lord reassuringly told him, "'My grace is sufficient for you, for My strength is made perfect in weakness.' Therefore most gladly I will rather boast in my infirmities, that the power of Christ may rest upon me" (2 Cor. 12:9).

MORE WEAPONS?

The current movements that emphasize signs, new revelations, and healings also often speak a great deal about spiritual warfare. Here again we need discernment.

Satan would have us go to extremes. Either we think too little about him, or we become preoccupied with him. Either we think we are out of range of his influence, or we imagine ourselves under constant bombardment. Either we are quick to blame Satan for emotional or physical problems, or we don't see him behind any problems. Either we think we're incapable of dealing with him, or we think he's afraid of us. Either we think we have no power against him, or we imagine that we have the power within ourselves to bad-mouth and bully him. But what does the Bible say?

How do human beings relate to the world of spirit beings?

The Bible says very little about the way we interact with angels and demons. It leaves little doubt that the spirit world and our physical world are interwoven in one reality, and that what happens in one realm influences what goes on in another. But God hasn't given us much information about the unseen world.

We do get glimpses of the angelic world as we read through the Bible. In the Old Testament, angels are often mentioned as the messengers of God and the ones who do God's bidding. And again in the New Testament we read of good angels as working invisibly to accomplish God's purposes in a world also inhabited by a host of wicked spirits under Satan's leadership.

The apostle Paul recognized the reality of the spirit world's influence on this world when he wrote,

We do not wrestle against flesh and blood, but against principalities, against powers, against the rulers of the darkness of this age, against spiritual hosts of wickedness in the heavenly places (Eph. 6:12).

And on the positive side, the author of Hebrews recognized the good angels as "spirits sent forth to minister for those who will inherit salvation" (Heb. 1:14). God's holy angels work for our good.

Bestselling Christian novels have dealt imaginatively with what the interaction might be between our world and the dark world of spirit beings. The books may be good literature, but they are not intended to be a source of good theology. And yet I have heard people talk as if those novels are accurate depictions of how the human and spirit worlds collide.

Then there are some religious leaders who suspect that demons lurk behind nearly every emotional or physical problem. They tell how they have conversed with demons and have cast out many demons from a person over several sessions.

However, except for the direct encounters that Jesus and the apostles had with demons as they cast them out of people, the Bible does not speak of such dramatic visible or audible interaction. It is significant that the letters of the New Testament do not contain instructions for exorcising demons, nor does the New Testament ever suggest that believers can be controlled by demons.

It is significant that the New Testament does not contain instructions for exorcising demons, nor does it ever suggest that believers can be controlled by demons.

Bible teacher R. C. Sproul discusses this issue in his book *Pleasing God*. He writes:

Within Christian circles there has arisen a new concern for ministries of deliverance. Some of these deliverance ministries have developed a bizarre and radically unbiblical view of demon possession and deliverance. . . . I have listened to tapes from well-known deliverance ministers in which they teach the signs of a departure of the demon. A sigh, for example, indicates the departure of the demon of tobacco. . . . There are demons for every conceivable sin. Not only must each one of these demons be exorcised, but there are necessary procedures to keep them from returning on a daily basis.

I know of no polite way to respond to this kind of teaching. It is unmitigated nonsense. Nowhere in sacred Scripture is there to be found the slightest hint of this kind of demonic diagnosis. These teachings cross the line into the sphere of magic and result in serious harm to believers who are duped by them. Sadly, too much concern with Satan and demons means that we focus less of our attention on Christ. That must please Satan, though it certainly is not pleasing to God. . . .

All this emphasis on Satan and demons tends to distract us from another very real menace, our own sin. . . . We cannot pass the blame and responsibility for our sin to a controlling demon. . . . We can say that we are tempted or incited or seduced by Satan, but not that we are controlled or coerced by him (*Pleasing God*, Tyndale House, 1988, pp.90-92).

How do Satan and his forces oppose God and His people?

Satan is our adversary (1 Pet. 5:8). His demons blind unbelievers to the truth (2 Cor. 4:4; 1 Tim. 4:1; Rev. 12:9). They influence people to make bad choices

(1 Chr. 21:1; Mt. 16:22-23; Lk. 22:3-4; Acts 5:3). They take control of some people (Mt. 8:28; 17:14-21). They somehow rule over and influence many national leaders (Dan. 10:10-21). They sometimes produce sickness and disease (Job 2:6-8; Mt. 9:32-33; 12:22; 17:15-19; Lk. 8:27-29; 13:11-17). They are the authors of heresy (1 Tim. 4:1-5; 2 Cor. 11:3,14; 1 Jn. 4:1-3).

What can we do in the spiritual battle?

Instead of inviting us to initiate direct confrontations with evil spirits, the Bible calls for us to choose allegiance to God and use the powerful spiritual weapons listed in Ephesians 6.

Stand therefore, having girded your waist with truth, having put on the breastplate of righteousness, and having shod your feet with the preparation of the gospel of peace; above all, taking the shield of faith with which you will be able to quench all the fiery darts of the wicked one. And take the helmet of salvation, and the sword of the Spirit, which is the word of God; praying always with all prayer and supplication in the Spirit (vv.14-18).

The armor includes:

The belt of truth—We must know the truth, affirm our belief in the truth, speak the truth, and respond to life's problems and challenges with the truth.

The breastplate of righteousness—We must choose to do what is right in God's eyes.

The shoes of the gospel of peace—This may refer to the reassurance that we are at peace with God, or perhaps it refers to readiness for action in His service at any time.

The shield of faith—We are to live by faith, continually choosing to trust God and not believe the lies of the enemy.

The helmet of salvation—We need to remember that our salvation is secure.

The sword of the Spirit—We must know and use God's Word.

The power of prayer—Although not a piece of armor as such, Paul emphasized the necessity of ongoing prayer. Through prayer we show our allegiance and submission to the Lord, and we lay hold of the strength that He desires to give to us.

In addition to what Paul wrote in Ephesians 6, the apostle Peter said:

> Be sober, be vigilant; because your adversary the devil
> walks about like a roaring lion, seeking whom he may
> devour. Resist him, steadfast in the faith, knowing that
> the same sufferings are experienced by your brotherhood
> in the world (1 Pet. 5:8-9).

Peter encouraged believers to stand firm and resist the devil. He knew all too well the powerful influence of Satan. Shortly after Jesus told Peter that Satan would "sift [him] like wheat" (Lk. 22:31), he denied the Lord three times (vv. 55-63).

James gave us similar instruction in his brief letter. He said, "Therefore submit to God. Resist the devil and he will flee from you" (4:7). James didn't give us an elaborate formula for fighting Satan's attacks. He didn't tell us to bad-mouth Satan or engage in the recitation of some key Christian phrases. He simply said to "resist" and Satan will flee.

After Jesus had spent 40 days in the wilderness, the devil came to Him and offered several temptations (Mt. 4:1-11). Jesus didn't do anything spectacular. He just quoted Scripture. He stated His allegiance to the will of the Father, reaffirmed the truth, and resisted Satan's lies.

Some may say that certain methods of dealing with demons must be right because they seem to work. But pragmatism is not proof. A method is not right simply because it seems to work. Even non-Christian religions and cults apparently have had success in casting out demons. One example found in the Bible is in Acts 19:13-16.

With the power of the Holy Spirit within us, we need to submit to God, trust in His strength, and let the devil know that we want nothing to do with him.

What are the basic truths to remember? By way of summary, here are some principles to remember:

- Rely on the Word of God.
- Don't derive your theology from experiences or what seems to work.
- Recognize the danger of attempting to communicate with demons.
- Recall that "He who is in you is greater than he who is in the world" (1 Jn. 4:4).
- Submit to the Lord.
- Resist Satan and he will flee.
- Pray always.
- Put on the armor God has provided.

GREAT EXPECTATIONS

In this age of the Spirit, God wants to work powerfully in and through us. He wants to transform us and make us more like Christ. His goal is to make us into Spirit-led, Spirit-filled ambassadors, helping people to find the liberating truth of the gospel and the joy of living for Christ. Individually and as churches we need to demonstrate the reality of the Spirit's power to transform lives.

To live that kind of life, though, we first need to be connected to the One who is the source of power, through faith in Jesus as our Savior and Lord (Jn. 3). When we accept His gift of forgiveness, the Spirit comes to live within us (1 Cor. 12:13; Rom. 8:9,15-16).

But that's not the end of the story. We do not live happily ever after without struggles and effort. We must daily say no to sin and yes to God (Rom. 6:11-13), submitting to the Lord and asking for the help of the indwelling Spirit of God (Eph. 5:18).

If we are daily depending on His Spirit, we will find the "something more" that we've been looking for. We can expect to experience the powerful work of the Spirit, finding joy and fulfillment as we learn from God's Word, asking in faith for both health and grace to endure, and depending on our spiritual armor to protect us from the evil one.

We can expect great things if we are depending on the Spirit.

FOUR

FREE IN THE SPIRIT

What can we do when we don't live up to our own principles? What if we find ourselves not doing what we want to do, while doing the very things we've determined not to do? These are not questions asked by someone trapped by an addiction. They're raised by a first-century writer who understood the realism and difficulty of spiritual struggle: the apostle Paul.

Many think of Paul as someone who lived above the common passions of life. His own words say otherwise. Nowhere do we find more realism than in the personal questions he raised in Romans, chapter 7. Nowhere can we find better solutions than in the answers he gave in chapter 8.

I hope you will better understand the way to greater spiritual freedom as you examine this brief study by Bill Crowder and the RBC writers.

Martin R. De Haan II

JEOPARDY:
A KEY TO BIBLE STUDY

In 1964 Merv Griffin sat in the dining room of his apartment and created a game called *Jeopardy*. Today his idea has grown into one of the most popular quiz shows in American television history. Over the years since then, show host Alex Trebek has challenged some 5,000 contestants with over 135,000 questions in as many as 2,700 categories of knowledge. One of the contestants, Frank Spangenberg, a New York City police officer, won $144,397.

Griffin gave *Jeopardy* an interesting twist by giving the answers and requiring contestants to come up with the right questions. In the *Jeopardy* tradition, a "question" might be: "This American author and humorist said, 'Denial ain't just a river in Egypt.'" The answer in *Jeopardy* is, "Who is Mark Twain?"

In Bible study, as in *Jeopardy*, there is benefit in looking not only for answers but also

> *In Bible study, as in* Jeopardy, *there is benefit in looking not only for answers but also for the right questions.*

for the right questions. The Word of God can seem irrelevant and lifeless until it is read with an awareness of the questions that bring the story line to life. Information about the pharaohs in Egypt may seem like backroom museum clutter until we begin asking questions that expose parallels in our own lives to the circumstances of people in ancient times.

In the following pages we will see how the answers

given in Romans 8, one of the most loved chapters in the Bible, match up with the questions that have plagued many of God's children throughout the centuries. The chapter begins with an uplifting statement:

Therefore, there is now no condemnation for those who are in Christ Jesus (8:1).

It also ends on a positive note:

I am convinced that neither death nor life . . . will be able to separate us from the love of God that is in Christ Jesus our Lord (8:39).

What is often forgotten, however, is the fact that the reassuring words of Romans 8 are a response to the questions raised by Paul's graphic and disturbing picture of his own spiritual struggle in chapter 7. Note his sadness and frustration:

I do not understand what I do. For what I want to do I do not do, but what I hate I do. . . . I know that nothing good lives in me, that is, in my sinful nature. For I have the desire to do what is good, but I cannot carry it out. For what I do is not the good I want to do; no, the evil I do not want to do—this I keep on doing (7:15,18-19).

At first these words do not seem to fit the apostle Paul, that courageous Christian who evangelized the first-century Roman world, wrote most of the New Testament epistles, and finally died as a martyr. But he is the man who penned these words, and he wrote it using the present tense. He was describing his inner struggle between his born-again self and a remaining inclination to evil that he called "the law of sin" (7:23). After describing this spiritual battle, he asked, "Who will rescue me from this body of death?" He responded with a jubilant exclamation: "Thanks be to God—through Jesus Christ our Lord!" But he knew this complete rescue would not take place until he was united with Christ: "So then, I myself in my mind am a slave to God's law, but in the sinful nature a slave to the law of sin" (7:25).

Paul knew that his complete rescue would not take place until he was united with Christ.

At this point we are likely to feel uneasy. We see too much of ourselves in this picture. We don't see ourselves as spiritual giants like Paul. He was assured of final victory, but what about us? We could understandably be asking questions like these:

1. If we keep failing, will God keep forgiving us?
2. Can we stop doing what we don't want to do?
3. Can we be sure God won't give up on us?
4. Is there a way out of this awful struggle?
5. Will God help us overcome the failures we experience every day?
6. Can anything separate us from the love of God?

Let's look now at each of these questions, which arise out of Paul's struggles in Romans 7. And then we'll see the answers he gives in Romans 8.

QUESTIONS & ANSWERS FROM ROMANS 7–8

In Romans 8, Paul gave us encouraging answers to questions raised in the previous chapter. However, he did not promise freedom from the struggle nor uninterrupted victory. He assured all of his readers, all those who are in Christ, that they would not lose their salvation nor lose all the battles along the way. We can be winners far more often than we will be losers.

QUESTION ONE:
If we keep failing, will God keep forgiving us?

ANSWER:
Yes, because He doesn't see us as we see ourselves. Paul began chapter 8 by assuring those who believe in Christ that they stand before God forgiven and accepted:

> *Therefore, there is now no condemnation for those who are in Christ Jesus, because through Christ Jesus the law of the Spirit of life set me free from the law of sin and death. For what the law was powerless to do in that it was weakened by the sinful nature, God did by sending His own Son in the likeness of sinful man to be a sin offering. And so He condemned sin in sinful man, in order that the righteous requirements of the law might be fully met in us, who do not live according to the sinful nature but according to the Spirit* (8:1-4).

The "therefore" points back to the exclamation of Romans 7:25, "Thanks be to God—through Jesus Christ our Lord!" Because of what Jesus Christ did in paying the full price for all our sins on the cross, we who have placed our trust in Him are free from the possibility of condemnation. So much for the fear of losing our salvation because of our failures! The term "in Christ," the statement about freedom from "the law of sin and death," and the declaration that "God sent His Son" contain the keys to understanding this wonderful Bible passage.

He sees us as "in Christ."

Those who believe in Christ no longer stand before God as guilty sinners. Instead, we stand before Him as "in Christ." This is an awesome truth! Jesus offered His sinless self to die on the cross, and in the process He took the death we deserve. We who believe are now so united with Him that we are described as being "in Christ." He is now in the heavenly realms exalted at God's right hand "far above all rule and authority, power and dominion, and every title that can be given" (Eph. 1:20-21). God has taken us who were spiritually dead, made us alive, and "raised us up with Christ and seated us with Him in the heavenly realms in Christ Jesus" (Eph. 2:6). We are now inseparably united with Him.

The fact that God sees us as being in Christ is one of the most inspiring truths of the Bible. To be "in Him" is to be accepted by God on the merits of Christ alone. In bookkeeping terms, this means that all our sin has been put into Christ's account, and all His goodness has been placed into our account. God's only requirement is that we trust in Christ. Our salvation is not found in good works, church attendance, an excellent reputation, or sacrificial religious acts of devotion—not even in making the Ten Commandments our standard of conduct! We are right with God only because we have received Jesus as Savior. When we did, God placed us in Christ.

He sees us as "free from the law."

Now let's look at the statement, "the law of the Spirit of life set me free from the law of sin and death" (8:2). What is this law of sin and death from which we have been set free? It is the good law of God, His rules for conduct, even the Ten Commandments. This answer shocks many religious people. They are trying to please God by keeping His laws, and here Paul said that we are free from these rules! Does this mean that we can now violate God's standards with impunity? Not at all!

What Paul was saying is that because of what Christ did for us, we have been freed from trying to keep the law to earn favor with God. The problem with trying to earn favor with God by following His rules is that we keep breaking them no matter how hard we try not to. The law,

The problem with trying to earn favor with God by following His rules is that we keep breaking them no matter how hard we try not to.

you see, tells us what to do but does not give us the power to do what it says. Even Paul had this problem. He said that the "law of sin" within him kept making him a lawbreaker (7:23). The law of God is good, but it can't help us because of our inclination toward sin. Trying to gain favor with God by keeping the law is an exercise in futility. It just keeps piling up our sins and increasing our guilt. Therefore, the law can do nothing except condemn us.

He sees us as people who have been rescued.

God did not give up on us. He provided a way to make us right with Him. Paul explained:

What the law was powerless to do in that it was weakened by the sinful nature, God did by sending His own Son in the likeness of sinful man to be a sin offering (8:3).

What could not be accomplished by the law, God did by coming to live among us. He came to earth in

> *God provided a way to make us right with Him.*

the person of Jesus. He came in the *likeness* of sinful man, not *as a* sinful man. He was like us in that He came in a body like ours, one that could get tired and suffer pain—not as a superman. Yet He was without sin. He was completely human, only sinless. Paul continued:

So He condemned sin in sinful man, in order that the righteous requirements of the law might be fully met in us, who do not live according to the sinful nature but according to the Spirit (8:3-4).

Jesus Christ, in our humanity, met the devil and sin on their own ground and defeated them. He died, never having sinned, to atone for our sins. He conquered death by His resurrection. Sin is now a dethroned tyrant whom we can overcome "through Christ Jesus the law of the Spirit of life" (8:2), who has set us free from the please-God-by-works routine.

QUESTION TWO:
Can we stop doing what we don't want to do?

ANSWER:
Yes, if we learn to rely on the Holy Spirit. In Romans 8:4, Paul introduced his readers to the concept of living "according to the Spirit" in contrast to living "according to the sinful nature." This is an important concept to understand. Let's look now at what Paul meant by living "according to the Spirit." And then we'll look at how we can do this.

We need to focus on what the Spirit desires.
This is what it means to live "according to the Spirit." It is to be "in step" with the Spirit —to follow His lead and remain under His control. If you are a believer, He is already in you for the purpose of leading and lovingly controlling you. Paul wrote:

Those who live according to the sinful nature have their minds set on what that nature desires; but those who live in accordance with the Spirit have their minds set on what the Spirit desires. The mind of sinful man is death, but the mind controlled by the Spirit is life and peace . . . . Those controlled by the sinful nature cannot please God. You, however, are controlled not by the sinful nature but by the Spirit, if the Spirit of God lives in you. And if anyone does not have the Spirit of Christ, he does not belong to Christ (8:5-9).

According to Paul, then, every person is either under the control of the Spirit or under the control of the old nature—either on the road that leads to life and peace or on the road that leads to death. Walking in step with the Spirit, therefore, is living with Him as the controller of our lives.

Now, this raises a problem. Many who belong to Christ have a lifestyle that does not appear to be very much under the control of the Holy Spirit. At times this is true of all of us. But if we truly received Jesus as our Savior, we did acknowledge Him as our Master, and our bodies became temples of the Holy Spirit (1 Cor. 6:19). And we are glad that we have been delivered from the tyranny of sin and death. However, we are having problems with ourselves. Some of our old ways still keep us from being what we know we ought to be. So how do we live under the Spirit's control? How do we stop doing what we don't want to do?

We need to consciously yield to the Spirit.

Paul addressed this issue many times in his letters. Again and again he stressed the matter of fully yielding ourselves to God. He did so in the 6th chapter of this letter to the believers in Rome. He said we are to consciously look upon ourselves as dead to our old way of life and offer every part of our lives to God (6:11-14). He said we must remember that we are under new management—that we were once "slaves to sin" but have been set free and are now "slaves to God" (6:15-23).

When Paul told the Ephesians not to get drunk with wine, but to "be filled with the Spirit" (Eph. 5:18), he was repeating this same theme: Yield to the Holy Spirit; consciously and continually give Him control of every area of life. As we do this, the fruit of the Spirit will become evident. Our lives will be marked by "love, joy, peace, patience, kindness, goodness, faithfulness, gentleness, and self-control" (Gal. 5:22).

We will never in this life reach the place where we will be perfectly satisfied with ourselves. In fact, the more we grow in likeness to Jesus, the more conscious we will become of our many continuing imperfections. But our imperfect way will end in victory.

We will never in this life reach the place where we will be perfectly satisfied with ourselves.

Our bodies, these weak tents that are so often the vehicles of failure, will one day be replaced by glorified bodies completely under the Spirit's control. Paul wrote this:

> *If Christ is in you, your body is dead because of sin, yet your spirit is alive because of righteousness. And if the Spirit of Him who raised Jesus from the dead is living in you, He who raised Christ from the dead will also give life to your mortal bodies through His Spirit, who lives in you (8:10-11).*

Living in step with the Spirit is walking on the path to life and peace—temporarily on earth, forever in heaven.

QUESTION THREE:
Can we be sure God won't give up on us?

ANSWER:
Yes, because God loves us as His children. Sensitive people, who are deeply conscious of their many failures because they too often allow their sinful nature to get the upper hand, may ask, "How can God keep accept-

ing me?" Paul answered this by assuring us that God is patient because we have been made members of His family. In Christ we have become God's children—His daughters and sons. Because of this father/child relationship, Paul assured the Roman believers that they didn't have to live in the kind of fear they had when they were trying to earn favor with God by works. They now had a new relationship with God. In Romans 8:12-17, Paul spoke of a new intimacy with God, a new source of assurance, and a new attitude toward suffering.

> *God is patient with us because we have been made members of His family.*

God encourages us to call Him "Daddy."

After repeating his strong warning that people who live under the domination of their sinful nature will die in their sins, Paul added:

> *But if by the Spirit you put to death the misdeeds of the body, you will live, because those who are led by the Spirit of God are sons of God. For you did not receive a spirit that makes you a slave again to fear, but you received the Spirit of sonship. And by Him we cry, "Abba, Father" (vv. 13-15).*

Yes, we have a high calling: to put to death the misdeeds of the body. But this is not a command to belittle ourselves or hate our bodies and their normal desires. It means rejecting those behaviors that are improper for a child of God. And because we are God's children, we must see all anxious fear as out of place. We parents would be hurt if our children lived in fear of us. So is God. He wants us to look upon Him as *Abba*, the term

Jewish children use for "Daddy." He proved His love for us in giving His Son to become our Savior through the humiliation and pain of the incarnation. He knows we are weak and frail and understands when we fail (Ps. 103:13-14). He stands always ready to forgive like a loving father and willing to help if we turn back to Him. For that reason, we can dismiss all anxious fear.

God assures us that we are His children.

As members of God's family indwelt by the Holy Spirit, we also have a new source of assurance—the constant witness of that same Spirit. We read, "The Spirit Himself testifies with our spirit that we are God's children" (8:16).

Some believers declare that they have absolute certainty about their salvation and their standing because God spoke to them in an audible voice. But they are a definite minority, and they are wrong if they think that an audible word from God is what Paul had in mind. The testimony of the Holy Spirit is an inner affirmation by the Spirit of God to our own spirit. John Wesley described it this way:

> *The testimony of the Holy Spirit is an inner affirmation by the Spirit of God to our own spirit.*

An inward impression on the soul, whereby the Spirit of God directly witnesses to my spirit that I am a child of God; that Jesus has loved me and given Himself for me; and that all my sins are blotted out, and I, even I, am reconciled to God (*Sermons I*, pp.124-125).

As we reflect on the wonder of all that God has done for us and yield ourselves to obey Him, our inner spirit responds to God in awe, worship, and adoration.

All of this is in beautiful harmony with a promise Jesus made on the eve of His crucifixion:

Whoever has My commands and obeys them, he is the one who loves Me. He who loves Me will be loved by My Father, and I too will love him and show Myself to him (Jn. 14:21).

How wonderful that this inner certainty is available to all believers, whether highly educated or barely able to read! A Christian scholar who had been educated in some of the most prestigious colleges and universities in the United States and Europe wrote a book on the witness of the Holy Spirit in which he pointed out that spiritual certainty must come from God. He knew all the philosophical arguments for the existence of God, the evidence for the authenticity of the Bible, and the reasons for belief in Jesus Christ. But he said that an uneducated believer could have an inner assurance just as strong as his. The witness of the Spirit of God with the human spirit has nothing to do with advanced scholarship. To use an old maxim in a new manner: It's not *how much* you know, but *Who* you know.

> *It's not* how much *you know, but* Who *you know.*

God calls us to look beyond our suffering.

Having the assurance of being sons and daughters of God changes our attitude toward all of life's circumstances. We begin to see everything from the perspective of eternity. Paul wrote:

Now if we are children, then we are heirs—heirs of God and co-heirs with Christ, if indeed we share in His sufferings in order that we may also share in His glory (8:17).

Christians who live in circumstances of affluence and liberty cannot fully appreciate this verse. But it had great significance for the Christians in Rome and for multitudes of persecuted and harassed believers through the ages. Participation with Christ in suffering during this life brings participation with Him in joy during the life to come!

> *Participation with Christ in suffering during this life brings participation with Him in joy during the life to come!*

Dietrich Bonhoeffer, the Lutheran pastor who dared oppose Hitler and was executed by the Gestapo just days before the Allied victory, believed this wholeheartedly. While in prison he wrote these words:

For while it is true that only the suffering of Christ Himself can atone for sin, and that His suffering and triumph took place "for us," yet to some, who are not ashamed of their fellowship in His body, He vouchsafes the immeasurable grace and privilege of suffering "for Him," as He did for them (From *Beacon Bible Commentary*, pp. 178-179).

To the degree that we participate in Christ's suffering, to that same degree we will revel in His glory. When we know this, we can suffer triumphantly.

QUESTION FOUR:
Is there a way out of this awful struggle?

ANSWER:
Yes, if we find ultimate hope in the life to come.
When we face troubles and trials, it is sometimes hard to keep from being discouraged. We trust God, but we wonder about the why of all the pain we and others around us must endure. At such times we may not enjoy deep inner peace, even though we have not abandoned our faith. During those times we need to take in the truths proclaimed in Romans 8:18-25, where Paul portrayed the created world first as in eager anticipation and then in the throes of childbirth.

We need to look forward to a re-created world.
Paul was able to be a complete optimist in the midst of pain and persecution because he focused on the glorious eternity that awaits God's children. He wrote:

> *I consider that our present sufferings are not worth comparing with the glory that will be revealed in us. The creation waits in eager expectation for the sons of God to be revealed. For the creation was subjected to frustration, not by its own choice, but by the will of the One who subjected it, in hope that the creation itself will be liberated from its bondage to decay and brought into the glorious freedom of the children of God* (8:18-21).

After declaring that our present pain is almost nothing when compared to our eternal glory, Paul personified the created world as waiting "on tiptoe" (J. B. Phillips) for the day when we humans will finally and fully become the children of God. Using the literary device of ascribing thought and feeling to nature, Paul said that the creation didn't choose to be the way it is, so marked by disaster, cruelty, and suffering. It is the way it is because of God's sentence of judgment that made nature a rod of discipline for sinful people. But God is planning a day when all such ugliness will be eradicated, and this great endtime event will occur in close connection with our glorification as the creatures God created to be His vice-regents over the earth.

Paul was able to be a complete optimist in the midst of pain and persecution because he focused on the glorious eternity that awaits God's children.

Francis Schaeffer, in his book on the Christian view of ecology, *Pollution And The Death Of Man*, encourages us to take up a long-neglected responsibility as a result of this promised restoration:

Biblical Christianity has a real answer to the ecological crisis. It offers a balanced and healthy attitude to nature, arising from the truth of its creation by God; it offers the hope here and now of substantial healing in nature of some of the results of the Fall, arising from the truth of redemption in Christ . . . . A Christian-based science and technology should consciously try to see nature substantially healed, while waiting for the future complete healing at Christ's return (p.81).

Interestingly, Paul depicted the natural world as knowing what scientists are just now beginning to realize. Today, many former agnostics are saying that the earth and the life in it are looking less and less like the products of blind chance. The astounding complexities discovered in the disciplines of physics and biology point to an original design that, by all appearances, had human life in view from the very beginning. This understanding, which they call "the anthropic principle," is new to them. But it is not new to us. We know it from the Bible, and we eagerly anticipate the time when God will restore the original glory of the creation (Acts 3:19-21).

We need to anticipate our new bodies.

Still thinking in terms of universal suffering in the present, Paul portrayed a universe and a redeemed people in the throes of childbirth:

> *We know that the whole creation has been groaning as in the pains of childbirth . . . . Not only so, but we ourselves, who have the firstfruits of the Spirit, groan inwardly as we wait eagerly for our adoption as sons, the redemption of our bodies. For in this hope we were saved (8:22-24).*

The created world is groaning as in childbirth because she will give birth to the new heavens and earth promised to us by God. We groan too as we wait for our new bodies, and we have good reason to wait with great expectation. We already have been given the "firstfruits of the Spirit." The particular word Paul used here is a strong metaphor, going beyond the idea of a down payment. Like the firstfruits offering in Israel, it is a specimen of what will follow in the full harvest. It is a foretaste of what awaits us. That is why we can sing these lines from an old hymn written by Charles Butler:

> *Once heaven seemed a far-off place,*
> *Till Jesus showed His smiling face;*
> *Now it's begun within my soul,*
> *'Twill last while endless ages roll.*

All of these wonderful truths, when understood and believed, will change our attitude toward suffering. We who have learned to say "Abba, Father" are assured that He has designed us for glory, and that suffering is a way of preparing us for this end. Having tasted His goodness, we look forward with a hope characterized in Scripture as "eager expectation."

QUESTION FIVE:
Will God help us overcome the failures we experience every day?

ANSWER:
Yes, He has promised to help and to intervene in our daily lives. Conscious of our weaknesses, inconsistencies, and repeated failures, we realize that we are often our own worst enemies. We want God's will, but we are also full of selfish desires. We wonder how God will protect us from ourselves. Paul answered this question by assuring us that God will step in and take care of us. In the person of the Holy Spirit, He will help us in our prayers. And as our heavenly Father, He will intervene in the circumstances of our lives.

He will help us in our prayers.
One of the areas where our weakness shows is in our

prayer life. Even when we pray, we are plagued by conflicting emotions. Selfish, sometimes even impure thoughts flash through our minds while we are talking to God. Sometimes we don't know what we should ask for. Sometimes we are so sick or weary that we can't do more than say, "Lord, please help me." How reassuring to know that God understands and that His Spirit makes sure our prayers are acceptable and effective. Paul wrote:

How reassuring to know that God understands and that His Spirit makes sure our prayers are acceptable and effective.

> In the same way, the Spirit helps us in our weakness. We do not know what we ought to pray for, but the Spirit Himself intercedes for us with groans that words cannot express. And He who searches our hearts knows the mind of the Spirit, because the Spirit intercedes for the saints in accordance with God's will (8:26-27).

It is the Holy Spirit who groans within us, and these groans are apparently wordless. Through these groans, as He labors to purify us in preparation for eternity, the Holy Spirit cleanses and revises the thoughts and desires of our hearts and presents them to God. The Father, who perfectly knows our hearts, receives these revised prayers and answers them. Paul perhaps had the intercessory ministry of the Holy Spirit in mind when he penned the doxology:

> Now to Him who is able to do immeasurably more than all we ask or imagine, according to His power that is at work within us, to Him be glory . . . for ever and ever! (Eph. 3:20).

He will work in all our circumstances for our good.
It is also comforting to know that even though we may
blunder and fail, God will intervene in our circumstances to make sure His purposes for us are realized.
Paul wrote:

We know that in all things God works for the good of
those who love Him, who have been called according to His
purpose. For those God foreknew He also predestined to be
conformed to the likeness of His Son, that He might be the
firstborn among many brothers. And those He predestined,
He also called; those He called, He also justified; those He
justified, He also glorified (8:28-30).

In these verses Paul's thoughts take in all eternity—
from the eternity before time began to the eternity after
time ends. In eternity past God made a number of
choices. The cosmos came into
existence by His choice. We live
as His image-bearers because He
chose to make us that way. We
are saved from our sins and destined for glory because God
loved us from before the foundation of the world and chose us as
His special people (Eph. 1:4-5).

God's eternal will is the reason for our existence and the
ground of our salvation. He is
not going to let anything prevent

> *We are saved
> from our sins and
> destined for glory
> because God loved
> us from before the
> foundation of the
> world and chose
> us as His special
> people.*

His will from being carried out to fulfillment—not the
schemes of the devil, not the strategies of God's enemies, not even the blunders and failures of His chil-

dren. Therefore Romans 8:28 is true! God will intervene when necessary to make sure that His purposes for us are realized. In all of life's circumstances God purposes to grow us up into Christ (Eph. 4:14-19) to prepare us for the day when we will be like Jesus, experiencing the reality expressed by the apostle John:

God will intervene when necessary to make sure that His purposes for us are realized.

> *Dear friends, now we are children of God, and what we will be has not yet been made known. But we know that when He appears, we shall be like Him, for we shall see Him as He is (1 Jn. 3:2).*

QUESTION SIX:
Can anything separate us from the love of God?

ANSWER:
No, nothing can change God's love for us. We have tendencies to be fickle, and we are surrounded by people with the same failing. Promises made today are often broken tomorrow. Popular songs are bestsellers for only a few weeks. Fashions keep changing. A sports figure may be a hero one day and a loser the next. Only God can be trusted to forever remain what He is now. Paul gloried in that and expressed his unbounded confidence that we never need to be afraid that His love may sometime end. First he pointed to the fact that God loves us so much that He didn't spare the life of His own Son on our behalf. Then he declared that

absolutely nothing in this universe is greater than God's love for us.

Nothing is greater than the sacrifice of God's Son.
Paul was exuberant as he thought of all God has done for us—especially the sacrifice of His one and only Son on our behalf:

What, then, shall we say in response to this? If God is for us, who can be against us? He who did not spare His own Son, but gave Him up for us all—how will He not also, along with Him, graciously give us all things? Who will bring any charge against those whom God has chosen? It is God who justifies. Who is he that condemns? Christ Jesus, who died— more than that, who was raised to life—is at the right hand of God and is also interceding for us (8:31-34).

God is for us! Moreover, His supreme demonstration of love in the past is proof of what He will do in the future. He who has bestowed on us His "unspeakable gift" will certainly not withhold lesser gifts. If God has acquitted us, how can any lesser being condemn us? If the Son of God, the Second Person of the eternal Trinity, died for us, broke death's power by resurrection, and is now at God's right hand making intercession for us, will God pay any attention to the charges brought by any other being—angel or devil? Impossible!

> *Absolutely nothing in this universe is greater than God's love for us.*

Nothing is greater than God's love for us.

Having shown the impossibility of anything changing God's plans for us, the apostle Paul pulled out all the stops and made a series of exulting declarations:

Who shall separate us from the love of Christ? Shall trouble or hardship or persecution or famine or nakedness or danger or sword? As it is written: For Your sake we face death all day long; we are considered as sheep to be slaughtered. No, in all these things we are more than conquerors through Him who loved us. For I am convinced that neither death nor life, neither angels nor demons, neither the present nor the future, nor any powers, neither height nor depth, nor anything else in all creation, will be able to separate us from the love of God that is in Christ Jesus our Lord (8:35-39).

These words say it all. They need no comment. Troubles from natural and supernatural opposing forces may assail us. But nothing in all the universe can defeat us! This was true in the first century. It is true now.

SUMMARY

QUESTION ONE:
If we keep failing, will God keep forgiving us?
Answer:
Yes, because He doesn't see us as we see ourselves.

QUESTION TWO:
Can we stop doing what we don't want to do?
Answer:
Yes, if we learn to rely on the Spirit.

QUESTION THREE:
Can we be sure God won't give up on us?
Answer:
Yes, because He loves us as His children.

QUESTION FOUR:
Is there a way out of this awful struggle?
Answer:
Yes, if we find ultimate hope in the life to come.

QUESTION FIVE:
Will God help us overcome the failures we experience every day?
Answer:
Yes, He has promised to help and intervene in our daily lives.

QUESTION SIX:
Can anything separate us from the love of God?
Answer:
No, nothing can change God's love for us.

Living Free In The Spirit

Pastor Bill Crowder relates this account of living in the light of Romans 8.

In 1995, on a trip to Moscow to train pastors, my teaching partner went to the classroom to begin a particular class session. When he got there, he discovered an unscheduled meeting taking place. The translator told him that the students had just learned that there was a bill before the Russian parliament that, if approved and signed, would outlaw the evangelical Baptist church. This was as it had been under Communism. When I arrived, we suspended teaching for a while, and talked about the threat of this proposal with our students. We expressed our deep concern for their safety.

We had gone to Russia with the thought that we were helping to train the next generation of Russian pastors, only to wonder whether we were training some of those who would become the next generation of Christian martyrs in Russia.

We spent more than 2 hours talking, weeping, and praying together, in which we shared our love and concern both for the church in Russia and the church in the West. At the end of the session, one of the students, Peter Zhirenkov, said this to me:

> "We are more than conquerors through Him who loved us."
> (ROM. 8:37)

"Thank you for caring for us, and thank you for loving us. But do not worry for us or our safety. You see, it is not enough for us to believe the gospel, and it is not enough for us to preach the gospel. It is necessary that we suffer for the gospel!"

What devotion! It is a devotion rooted in the confidence that none of the struggles, battles, or adversities of life can in any way hinder or diminish the love of Christ for us. This confidence makes God's people "more than conquerors through Him who loved us."

That is living free in the Spirit